The Blueprint Projects

Making the Bible personal, relatable,
becoming a true Prophetess

April Zahlmann and Jackie Johnson

WestBow
PRESS®
A DIVISION OF THOMAS NELSON
& ZONDERVAN

WestBow Press books may be ordered through booksellers or by contacting:

WestBow Press
A Division of Thomas Nelson & Zondervan
1663 Liberty Drive
Bloomington, IN 47403
www.westbowpress.com
1 (866) 928-1240

Illustrated by Nayla S'mone

ISBN: 978-1-6642-0048-7 (sc)
ISBN: 978-1-6642-0047-0 (e)

Library of Congress Control Number: 2020913979

Print information available on the last page.

WestBow Press rev. date: 09/30/2020

A special thank you:
We would like to thank our husbands, Darrick Zahlmann and Shane Johnson
for believing in us. We are grateful for your love, support, and wisdom.

To our artist – Nayla S'mone:
Thank you for your hard work and creativity. God has truly kissed your hands.
Your talent takes our breath away. Your heart, passion and individuality set you
apart as an artist, never let anyone steal that from you. We thank you for blessing
our book with your artistry. You brought our vision alive and knew exactly how to
create every image we asked of you. Thank you from the bottom of our hearts.

Session 1

The Bible is God's living word; it is alive and will speak truth into your life. It gives you all the tools you need to grow in Jesus, live a Christian life, and deny Satan by covering yourself in the complete armor of God.

—Ephesians 6:10–18

The Blueprint Projects (BP) will help make the Bible relatable to your own personal life. Does the Bible intimidate you? Do you know scripture verses? Do you read some books in the Bible but feel desperate to know the whole story? Do you want to know more? Do you have a tug in your heart to understand how this book—the living word and truth of God—relates to your life?

With *The Blueprint Projects*, we are going to travel on a journey together learning about the Bible, digging into the Ten Commandments, and making this beautiful history book completely relatable to each of you. After this study, you will have created a blueprint for your life. You can take this design, or plan, with you wherever you go and refer to it on a continual basis. Your Bible will be your truth, and your blueprint will be your journal. It will be beautiful, stunning, personal, and designed by you. It is about your life, your struggles, your joys, your confusions, and your love—all related to scripture with Jesus in the perfect center.

Are you ready? Let's get started.

The Blueprint Projects Rules

- Honesty: Be completely honest with yourself. This process will not work if you aren't digging into your heart and pouring out your truth.

- Dedication: You have to commit to complete each session. You will miss a very important step if you miss even one session. Life happens, but we strongly encourage you to go through any sessions you miss or allow yourself the time to complete the sessions in order.
- Autonomy: This is completely private, is not to be shared, and is for your eyes only. The only exception to this rule is during discussion time if you feel God is leading you to share something. Please be very prayerful about what you share.
- Diligence: Complete each personal journaling time. In order to successfully move through this journey, the journaling must be completed.
- Nonjudgment: We are not here to judge or condemn you. Every person in the history of humankind—even the people in the Bible, except Jesus—has good and bad. If we are honest, the BP will open our eyes to our sinful nature and empower us to make a change toward a Christlike life.
- Redemption: We are not here to go through every sin with you. Jesus wants to redeem you from sin. Your personal Blueprint will be looking at your heart and not just the sin.
- Safety: Questions! If you are completing this in a group, we want all your questions. Don't be shy about asking questions during this process: personal questions, biblical questions, or anything that may be bothering you. The goal is for you to truly know God and his love for you. We don't want uncertainty on a certain topic to get in your way. Your coaches are here to help you build a deeper, more intimate relationship with Jesus. We will come by your side and help you find peace with some of the difficult questions you may have. If you are completing BP on your own, we encourage you to reach out to a strong believer of Christ to confirm what you are hearing or answer questions you may have.
- Design: This Blueprint is yours. Be creative. Add color and illustrations. Make this project your own personal journal.
- Owner's manual: The Blueprint is not a book of rules to follow to prove your loyalty or worthiness to God. This is an owner's manual for your life. This process is going to be tough. It is direct. Some areas will impact you harder than the rest, but God's grace is with you. We are here to grow in the Lord and build a closer relationship with Jesus.

As of today, we are moving forward! Let's begin by tackling a couple of logistical questions. It is perfectly okay if you don't know the answers to the questions below. Answer them to the best of your ability. We are here to learn, grow, and live for Jesus. We don't need to know everything; we just need to have open hearts, be respectful, and be willing to learn.

In your own words, explain what it means to be a follower of Jesus Christ. Do you see Jesus as your one true God or as a historical figure? Remember to use complete honesty here. What do you think it means to be a follower of Christ? Do not say what your church says, what your parents tell you, or what your pastor has told you. Make this personal.

Briefly define the word *sin* and what it means to you.

In the Bible, sin is described as an immoral act against God's law or against God's commands.

Do you know what the Trinity is?

The Trinity is the state of being three. In the Bible, the Trinity includes God, Jesus, and the Holy Spirit—one God in three divine persons. We have God, our Father. He sent his Son, Jesus Christ, who died on a cross for our sins. We then receive the gift of the Holy Spirit when we accept Jesus into our hearts as our Lord and Savior.

What is your definition of the Gospel?

The Gospel is defined as the record of Jesus's life and teachings in the first four books of the New Testament: Matthew, Mark, Luke, and John.

In the book of Matthew, Jesus is speaking to his disciples about salvation. Let's learn through Jesus, including what he says about salvation and taking up the cross.

> When the disciples heard this, they were greatly astonished, saying, "Who then can be saved?" But Jesus looked at them and said, "With man this is impossible, but with God all things are possible." Peter answered them, "We have left everything to follow you! What then will there be for us?" Jesus said to them, "Truly, I tell you, at the renewal of all things, when the Son of Man sits on his glorious throne, you who have followed me will also sit on twelve thrones, judging the twelve tribes of Israel. And everyone who has left houses or brothers or sisters or fathers or mother or wife or children or fields for my sake will receive a hundred times as much and will inherit eternal life. But many who are first will be last, and many who are last will be first." (Matthew 19:25–30)

Discussion Time

With your group, briefly discuss what this verse means to you. Jot down your thoughts.

What stands out? Go through your thoughts now and underline any verse that stood out to you.

Let this verse sink into your skin and into your heart, and carry it with you throughout the entire Blueprint projects. Let's take up the cross and follow Jesus. Let's make his teaching personal to our hearts and to our lives. Our walk with Jesus depends on this.

Jesus died on the cross and rose again three days later so we all can be saved. Through Jesus Christ, our sins are forgiven; they were left at the foot of the cross.

For the gifts and the calling of God are irrevocable. (Romans 11:29)

The one who is victorious will, like them, be dressed in white. I will never blot out the name of that person from the book of life, but will acknowledge that name before my Father and his angels. (Revelation 3:5)

For God so loved the world that he gave his one and only Son, that whoever believes in him shall not perish but have eternal life. For God did not send his Son into the world to condemn the world, but to save the world through him. (John 3:16–17)

I am the good shepherd; I know my sheep and my sheep know me—just as the Father knows me and I know the Father—and I lay down my life for the sheep. I have other sheep that are not of this sheep pen. I must bring them also. They too will listen to my voice, and there shall be one flock and one shepherd. (John 10:14–16)

[Jesus says,] "I give them eternal life, and they shall never perish; no one will snatch them out of my hand. My Father, who has given them to me, is greater than all; no one can snatch them out of my Father's hand. I and the Father are one." (John 10:28–29)

The Bible provides proof that nothing can snatch you from our Father's hand. God is our comforter, our provider, and our protector. He loves us with a love that is far greater than anything we have ever experienced.

When we come to know Jesus and invite him into our hearts, we need to take action. We must make changes in our lives that reflect who Jesus is—and not what this earth is. Sometimes, that means taking things out of our lives, including television shows, books, people, and anyone or anything that is distracting us or separating us from Jesus. Through this process, we will learn how to create a plan to set up boundaries while still shining Jesus's love on all our neighbors. We will learn how to be still and listen to what Jesus is asking us to do to win people for his kingdom. In every season of life, Jesus will call you to new and different roles, and he will perfectly place you to be his light.

> In the same way, faith by itself, if it is not accompanied by action, is dead. But someone will say, "You have faith, I have deeds." Show me your faith without deeds, and I will show you my faith by my deeds. You believe that there is one God. Good! Even the demons believe that—and shudder. (James 2:17)

> You see that his (Abraham) faith and his actions were working together, and his faith was made complete by what he did. (James 2:22)

> Our prayer is that through this project, you will hear from Jesus and your faith will be ignited by seeing who he wants you to be, what he wants you to do, and when, where, and what action he needs you to take for him. Jesus wants your heart, give him your heart and he will give you plans to prosper you, a future and a hope. (Jeremiah 29:11).

With God's great love, we also need to become aware of what repentance is. Repentance is the act of confessing our sins and asking for forgiveness:

> If we claim to be without sin, we deceive ourselves and the truth is not in us. (1 John 1:8)

> If we claim we have not sinned, we make him out to be a liar and his word is not in us." (1 John 1:10)

When we walk with Jesus, through the Holy Spirit, we become more aware of our sins. It is biblical that we must humble ourselves and turn from our wicked ways, and when we take communion each week, we must repent of our sins.

If my people, who are called by my name, will humble themselves and pray and seek my face and turn from their wicked ways, then I will hear from heaven, and I will forgive their sin and will heal their land. (2 Chronicles 7:14)

If we confess our sins, he is faithful and just and will forgive us our sins and purify us from all unrighteousness. (1 John 1:9)

Before we answer the question below, from the verses above in John 10, please underline the section where it says "my sheep know me and listen to my voice."

Put on the full armor of God, so that you can take your stand against the devil's schemes. (Ephesians 6:11)

Take the helmet of salvation and the sword of the Spirit, which is the Word of God. (Ephesians 6:17)

From what we underlined in John 10, Jesus says, "My sheep know me, they listen to my voice."

So, how do we know Jesus? How do we hear his voice? How do we stand against the schemes of the devil as Ephesians 6:11 mentioned?

Your sword is the Word of God (Ephesians 6:17). Your sword is your Bible! Your fighting tool is your Bible! The Bible is God's living Word. We learn his Word; we learn his truth, and we can hear from the Spirit because the Holy Spirit lives in your hearts. Through repentance, we are forgiven, we are healed, our hearts are opened, and we can hear Jesus. Through Jesus Christ, when you accept him as your Lord and Savior, you get to walk with the Spirit living inside you. It is the best gift you will ever receive.

Based on everything we have just learned, what are some of the things you can do now and throughout your life to ensure you stay close to Jesus and never lose intimacy with God? Refer to the verses above. Jot down your thoughts. Make a list.

Salvation comes through Jesus. It is secure. No one can snatch you from Jesus, but this does not mean we can get lazy. This does not mean we can get complacent. We have to hear Jesus; we have to know him and hear his voice (John 10). We do this through a sharp sword (Ephesians 6). Your sword sharpens every day you are in God's Word. I don't know about you, but I love a sharp sword! Nothing is better than a sharp knife. A dull sword makes you tired, it makes you weak, it makes you fall, and it makes you want to throw the sword away. A sharp sword or a sharp knife brings life, it cuts precisely, and it brings forth the best cuts of meat and the best cuts of bread.

Going through *The Blueprints Projects* is going to make your sword strong! We want to congratulate you ladies for saying yes to BP and for longing to deepen your faith in Jesus Christ.

You are making a physical action to publicly show how much you love Jesus!

> A sluggard's appetite is never filled, but the desires of the diligent are fully satisfied. (Proverbs 13:4)

You ladies are richly supplying your future!
Now that we have a grasp on salvation and the love of Jesus, let's head over to Deuteronomy 5, The Ten Commandments, and read its entirety.

The Ten Commandments are laws given to us by God, through Moses, to show us that humans fall short of the glory of God. We live in a sinful world, and God knows we have struggles. He knows we are confused, we have questions, and we have temptations. God gave us the Ten Commandments to help us see the things we need to work on in life.

When you look into the mirror, you see your flaws. You can't understand why you don't see beauty—or maybe you only see beauty with makeup on. You start to think, *How does Jesus see beauty in me? God made me in his image but from an earthly perspective, I don't fit what culture deems as beautiful.* You feel sad. You feel lost. So, you decide to do something about it.

By looking in the mirror, you can see yourself. You might need to start working out, start brushing your hair in the morning, or stop trying to be someone who is not really you. The mirror allows you to see your face, your body, and your physical appearance. Think of the Ten Commandments as a mirror. It is God's mirror.

As we go through the Ten Commandments, we can start seeing situations in our hearts that we need to change and situations we don't need to change. By looking into God's mirror, we begin to refine ourselves. We can start seeing less of us and more of the image of Christ. The Ten Commandments are not just laws or rules to follow to show our loyalty or worthiness to God; they are a beautiful guide that God gave us to follow so we can be more like him and to keep us closely connected to him.

Blessings for Obedience

> If you fully obey the Lord your God and carefully follow all his commands I give you today, the Lord your God will set you high above all the nations on earth. All these blessings will come on you and accompany you if you obey the Lord your God. (Deuteronomy 28:1–2)

The Blueprint Projects is not a study just of the Ten Commandments. The Ten Commandments will take you on a journey to discover who you really are in Christ. We will be combining scripture from the Old Testament and the New Testament.

Our prayer is this study will challenge you to dig into relevant topics that will change your life so you can leave an imprint in this world. This is only possible if you are brave enough to step into the woman who God has called you to be.

Let's take a step forward today. Let's bridge the gap between the Bible and your personal life. Let's create an intimate relationship with Jesus Christ so we can leave a beautiful legacy.

As we close, let's personalize this verse from John 10:14 by inserting your name in the blanks and trying to commit this verse to memory:

> Jesus says, I am the good shepherd. I know _____, and _____ knows me—just as the Father knows me and I know the Father—and I lay down my life for _____.

You are so loved, sweet sister.

Prayer

> Dear Jesus,
> Thank you for this opportunity to work through The Blueprint Projects. Thank you for my friends and these leaders. Jesus, please open my heart, mind, and eyes to your truths. Let me be honest, open, and able. Show me who you want me to be! Let me see a glimpse of myself the way you see me, dear Jesus. Let me connect with you deeper and deeper each day and each week.
>
> Jesus, I know that you know me. I know you love me. I know you laid down your life for me. I know nothing can snatch me from you and your love. Thank you! Today—and every day going forward—change my

heart and mind where it needs to be changed. Give me the courage to
move forward in every way you ask me to. Whisper in my ear everything
I need to receive from this.
In your heavenly name! Amen.

Personal Journal Time

Journal about the following questions on the pages below:

- Who am I right now? Be specific. Include name, passions, interests, characteristics
  that define you, personal beliefs, dreams, and goals. Get personal.
- What do I stand for? It's okay to be broad here and then pray to God and allow
  him to lead you to dig a bit deeper. We want you to get raw with God and
  yourself.
- What am I willing to fight for? What laws and rules are sealed in your heart?
  Are you willing to lay down your life for your faith? Are you willing to lay down
  your life for Jesus?

Note: As you complete your journaling, you do not need to fill up all the pages we
give you. The purpose of your BP is to always have it with you to turn to in times of
struggles, praise, doubts, and growth. It's good to keep some of your pages blank so
in three months, six months, one year, five years, or even ten years from now, you can
still turn to this, write in it, and grow in your walk with Jesus. Don't forget to date your
journaling! Fill your journaling with scriptures, verses, stories, drawings, and people
in the Bible who stand out to you. Let God's truth guide you.

Pray: As you begin to journal about these questions, remember the scripture you have
learned so far and dig into prayer as you write. Each day, pray over your Blueprint and
ask God to open your heart to hear him and know him on a deeper level. Jesus is right
here with you. He is helping you make his story, his history, and his heart personable
to yours.

❧ *Personal Journal Time: Session 1*

As you begin your journaling, remember to begin with a prayer. Invite the Holy Spirit in, refer to all the questions from this session to help guide you, become vulnerable, and add scriptures!

Questions for Guidance

- Who am I right now? Be specific … include name, passions, and interests, characteristics that define you, personal beliefs, dreams, and goals. Get personal.
- What do I stand for? It's okay to start broad here, then pray to God and allow him to lead you to dig a bit deeper. We want you to get raw with God and yourself.
- What Am I willing to fight for? What laws and rules are sealed in your heart? Are you willing to lay down your life for your faith? For Jesus?

Apple Blossom

Session 2

The Ten Commandments

In fact, this is love for God: to keep his commands.
And his commands are not burdensome.
—1 John 5:3

Commandment 1

I am the Lord your God, who brought you out of Egypt, out of the land of slavery. You shall have no other gods besides me.
—Deuteronomy 5:6–7

Commandment 2
You shall not make for yourself an image in the form of anything in heaven above or on the earth beneath or in the waters below. You shall not bow down to them or worship them.
—Deuteronomy 5:8–10

As we begin our journey, we want to emphasize the importance of learning our Bible and becoming familiar with using it. I want you to close your eyes right now, breathe, and think about who Jesus is. Do you know him? Do you know his love? Can you feel his peace, his goodness, his passion of greatness for you, his kindness, his gentleness, his faithfulness to you, his self-control, and the patience he has for you?

Jesus is love. When Jesus walked this earth, if you touched him, you were healed.

When he sat down in the grass, children flocked to him, sat in his lap, and immediately felt and breathed in his agape love. When Jesus died for you, he gave you the gift of the Holy Spirit. This means he wants to live inside you and never leave you again.

When you accept Jesus as your Lord and Savior, you are given the Spirit to dwell and live inside your heart and soul. However, it's your job to ignite the Spirit. You see, a person can accept Jesus but never ignite the Spirit of Jesus inside her.

As your eyes are closed, pray about igniting his Spirit during this study. Pray about ways you can learn Jesus on a deeper level. How can you personalize him to your everyday life? How can you begin a more intimate relationship with him? What do you need to remove from your life to grow your relationship with Jesus?

If you aren't quite sure who Jesus is, this is your chance to start learning who he is and what he is all about. Your walk with Jesus is about a relationship. Let's start right now by forming your relationship, building it, and falling in love with Jesus.

He is ready! Ladies, let's ignite the power of the Holy Spirit today.

Together, let's open to Isaiah 44:13–20.

Write down how you think this verse relates to today's times and your life in particular.

Reflection Time

- What is your definition of idolatry?

- What are your top three passions?

- What are the top three things you obsess over?

- What are the top three things you love to do?

- How is the thing you obsess over keeping you from experiencing freedom or holding you back in some way, be honest with yourself, this book is for you!

Idolatry is defined as the worship of a physical object as a god, an immoderate attachment, or a devotion to something. In the Old Testament, God talks about idolatry and worshipping other Gods.

Let's look at Jonah 2:8, which explains how God feels about worshipping idols.

Pull out your Bible and jot down this verse; if you are able to, write down this verse in more than one version and review.

Jonah 2:9 states:

> But I, with shouts of grateful praise, will sacrifice to you. What I have vowed, I will make good. I will say, "Salvation comes from the Lord."

Okay, let's take idolatry and look at it in today's times. God doesn't want us to worship gods, but it goes further than this. Looking back at the obsessions you listed, which ones fall into the category of what was described in the verses in Jonah? What earthly things are you sacrificing attention, time, and energy for that could be used to increase your relationship with Jesus?

Is it a friend who you're comparing yourself to? Do you want a boyfriend? A husband? Will you completely break down if your life doesn't go as planned? What social media account do you find yourself going to every day? When you want to find an outfit to wear, where do you go? When life gets hard, what is your natural instinct? Do you go to a friend's social media account or shop at a particular store that you love? Do you fall into the trap of comparison? We ask you to be honest here. What thoughts and/or actions in your life take up most of your time?

Remember Eve's original sin in Genesis 3? She did not trust that God had picked out the best intention and life for her. Another way of saying this is anything that cheats you of what God has for you could lead to sin.

These questions we ask are not bad in moderation, but if we aren't careful, we can find ourselves worshipping something that isn't aligned with God's will for our lives. We need to set boundaries with our time. Are you spending more time on things that really don't matter in life than on investing in your relationship and knowledge of God and Jesus?

Think about the definition of worship for a moment. To worship is "to regard with great or extravagant respect, honor, or devotion; a celebrity worshipped by her fans." Worshipping things of this world can quickly turn into a life filled with Idolatry, which means our love is being channeled in the wrong direction.

What are you worshipping? These are important questions to ask yourself and reflect on as you step into your role in Christ and your role as the woman Christ is calling you to be. Jot down your thoughts.

Eve's original sin stemmed from wanting more than the blessings God had given her and listening to Satan's lies. In her disobedience, she listened to Satan's lies instead of focusing on God's love for her. Love is defined as "an intense feeling of deep affection, tenderness, warmth, intimacy, compassion, sympathy, worship, concern, and unselfishness."

If we want a culture of change, then pure agape love is the one thing that can provide the greatest impact to Christian culture today. We live in a culture that continually wants more, which can bring us a life that is outside God's path for us.

In our world today, Satan has successfully targeted the biggest weakness in the women's soul, through television, social media, and images in magazines. These outlets target the female's biggest weakness, which makes her think she can have more and that she deserves more.

Jesus contradicts this cultural fallacy in the Great Commandment:

> "Teacher, which is the greatest commandment in the Law?" Jesus replied:
> "'Love the Lord your God with all your heart and will all your soul and

with all your mind.' This is the first and greatest commandment. And second is like it: 'Love your neighbor as yourself.' All the Law and the Prophets hang on these two commandments." (Matthew 22:36–40)

Satan's number one objective is to distract you from God's plan for you. He uses distractions, feelings, and relationships to derail you from what God has for you! God loves you and created you for something so unique and special.

As we step into this new role, we have to start molding our hearts, minds, and souls for a walk of love instead of a walk of constantly wanting more.

If we believe that our beauty comes from the love of God, then imagine the impact we could have on our culture today. We have the Spirit inside of us, which gives us the power to share this pure agape love everywhere we go. As women for Jesus, we need to stop peeking around at what other women are wearing and comparing ourselves with them. We need to stop idolizing other women's families or all the things they have.

Every morning, we need to wake up, pray to God and choose to walk in complete love and peace, knowing our relationship with Jesus is firm. We don't need to judge, compare, or want more because we hold God in our hearts. We are strong. We are confident. We are women who are called by God to do great things.

To walk this way daily is hard. There is no way around that. Cover your life in scripture, carry note cards with scripture on them everywhere you go, constantly speak Jesus's name, and ask for help with your words and actions. We can do this together!

To help, we have provided note cards at the end of your BP with each session's personalized verses for you cut out, read, pray over, and place all over your life. Keep them next to your bed, in your bathroom, in your car, or in your purse. Cover your life in scripture.

Reflection Time

How would you define your love here on earth? Be honest. This is not what you think love is; define love as you know it. When you say or hear the word *love*, what does it mean to you? Who comes to your mind when you think about love and the people you love in your life?

Let's journey through the scriptures to see what God says love is. When reading, take note that *vain* means "useless, producing no result," and toil means "to work extremely hard, exhausting physical labor."

Psalm 127: A Song of Ascents of Solomon

> Unless the Lord builds the house, the builders labor in vain.
> Unless the Lord watches over the city, the guards stand watch in vain.
> In vain you rise early and stay up late,
> toiling for food to eat—for he grants sleep to those he loves.
> Children are a heritage from the Lord, offspring a reward from him.
> Like arrows in the hands of a warrior are children born in one's youth.
> Blessed is the man whose quiver is full of them.
> They will not be put to shame when they contend with their opponents
> in court.

This psalm has multiple layers to it; let's study this verse with the thought that we are God's children—and God is the parent. God breathed into us and gave us life. How blessed is God with all of us children loving and respecting him?

The word *grant* means "to give or provide something." We learn that God gives sleep and rest to those he loves. Research the meaning of *giving*. Write down all your thoughts.

Your BP process helps you dig deep into God's role in your life. Are you willing to put God in the center of your life? Are you willing to say God is your lifeline? Through this BP journey, our prayer is for you to publicly pronounce God as the builder of your house and your life! God has given us the free choice to build our lives on our own merit, but throughout history, we can see that never works out for good.

God enjoys giving you blessings, loving you, and giving you rest, but you have to be a blessing to receive a true blessing. Today, let's proclaim that God is the true builder of our lives. Let's acknowledge that we are completely dependent on him. Let's pray daily for our eyes and hearts to be open so we can be a blessing on God and our neighbors.

Let's humble ourselves and truly believe God made—and is making—everything in our lives.

When and/or if we have been hit with trials or pain, we proclaim that God is still the builder of our lives and will make everything bad for good.

Let's move forward today. When we do this, our enemies don't stand a chance against us! Hallelujah!

Did you know the Bible was written in Hebrew? Did you know the very first language that the Bible was translated to was Greek?

The Hebrew translation of the word *love* is *Ahava*, which is broken down to three parts:

- Ahh: God exhaled.
- Hahn: Man inhales.
- Vahn: Love came.

The root word of ahava is "ahav," which means "to give" in Hebrew. Pure ahava, true love, is completely about giving and not receiving. Giving is the vehicle of love. To truly give with thought, consideration, and devotion is not an emotion but an action. Giving is often a form of sacrifice. The more you give to the person you love, the deeper the connection.

In the beginning, God gave us the gift of life—and then he gave us the ultimate gift of his Son. There is no deeper connection and no bigger gift. The first letter in the word Ahava is the Hebrew letter "Aleph." Aleph means Father in the Hebrew language. It represents the beginning from which all things are created. In the beginning, God created the heavens and the earth for us. What a gift!

As we close, let's personalize Psalm 127:1–2 by inserting your name in the blanks. Try to commit this verse to memory:

> Unless the Lord builds _____'s house, the builders labor in vain. Unless the Lord watches over _____'s city, the guards stand watch in vain. In vain you rise early and stay up late, toiling for food to eat—for he grants sleep to _____, whom he loves.

Personal Journal Time

Look up these verses, write them down, and pray over them as you begin your journaling for the week:

- Exodus 20:3
- Isaiah 44:8
- Isaiah 45:56
- Acts 4:12
- 1 John 5:21

Journal about the following questions:

- Now that you have a deeper understanding of love, how do you want to show love to your family, friends, future husband, and kids?
- How will you accept love from others now that you have had time to think about the true beauty and gift of love?
- Who are you in Christ? As you enter the world with Christ as your center, what morals and standards of living do you want to stick by?
- Who do you want to be in Christ? What characteristics about your life do you want to stay with you as you enter the world? What gifts has God given you so far?
- What has God given you in your life so far? Write down and/or draw the blessings and miracles God has given you. Let's celebrate the goodness of Jesus.
- What are your idols? Dig deep here. What things, people, and places are you turning to instead of immediately turning to God first?

It's so important to journal, write, or draw. Your BP is becoming an owner's manual for your life. Even though we struggle with idols, we may be currently carrying them around like a heavy weight, but because of Jesus and his sacrifice—his agape love for us—we get to break free from these idols.

Let's break free this week.

Prayer

Write a prayer specific to your own life. Here is how to get started:

> God take these idols from me. Take these struggles and sin from me.
> Redeem me. I am yours. I am loved. I am chosen. I am a child of God.
> Guide me to a deeper relationship with you. Amen.

As your coaches, we pray that you take this very seriously. It is so important that today—and this week—you truly dig into who you are, what you want to stand for, and who you want to become as you age. We are on your side. We have become prayer warriors for you! We will be praying that God leads you on a journey toward a deeper love and passion for him. He helps you break free from whatever is holding you back: your idols, your temptations, your insecurities, and your faults. We all have them, but we are all daughters of our one true King—and we are so very loved by him. Let him help you.

ℰ *Personal Journal Time: Session 2*

As you begin your journaling, remember to begin with a prayer. Invite the Holy Spirit in and refer to all the questions from this session to help guide you, become vulnerable, and add scripture!

Questions for Guidance

- Now that you have a deeper understanding of love, how do you want to show love to your family, friends, future husband, and kids?
- How will you accept love from others now that you have had time to think about the true beauty and gift of love?
- Who are you in Christ? As you enter the world with Christ as your center, what morals and standards of living do you want to stick by?
- Who do you want to be in Christ? What characteristics about your life do you want to stay with you as you enter the world? What gifts has God given you so far?
- What has God given you in your life so far? Write down and/or draw the blessings and miracles God has given you. Let's celebrate the goodness of Jesus.
- What are your idols? Dig deep here. What things, people, and places are you turning to instead of immediately turning to God first?

Almond Flower

Session 3

Commandment 3

You shall not misuse the name of the Lord your God, for the Lord
will not hold anyone guiltless who misuses his name.
—Deuteronomy 5:11

This week, let's dig into the word *blasphemy*, which is defined as the act or offense of speaking sacrilegiously (sinful, disrespectful, unholy) about God or sacred things; profane/ungodly talk. As a group, quickly look up synonyms and share them with each other. Write down a couple.

Now, let's take a look in the mirror. What do you say on a daily, weekly, or monthly basis that you feel is offensive to God? Write it down. Be completely honest. In order to be redeemed, we need to get raw and dig into the sensitive, somewhat embarrassing actions we say or do.

We forget that God is right here with us, right now. Unlike the friend everyone is talking about behind their back, God can hear you disrespecting him. Can you imagine the pit in your stomach if you overheard someone you loved deeply insulting you in the most offensive way possible? Jot down a little bit how you would feel. God hears you every time you say anything offensive or disrespectful.

We are now going to learn about taming the tongue from the New Testament book of James.

Did you know that James was Jesus's brother? He was a servant of God and Jesus Christ. He felt very strongly that we, as Christians, should live out what we say we believe. At first, James was hesitant to believe in Jesus Christ (John 7:5), but he eventually surrendered his life to Jesus Christ and was called a man of faith, a "pillar" of the church (Galatians 2:9).

Taming the Tongue

As you read James 3:1–12, underline and/or highlight any verses that stick out to you:

> Not many of you should become teachers, my fellow believers, because you know that we who teach will be judged more strictly. We all stumble in many ways. Anyone who is never at fault in what they say is perfect, able to keep their whole body in check. When we put bits into the mouths

of horses to make them obey us, we can turn the whole animal. Or take ships as an example. Although they are so large and are driven by strong winds, they are steered by a very small rudder wherever the pilot wants to go. Likewise, the tongue is a small part of the body, but it makes great boasts. Consider what a great forest is set on fire by a small spark. The tongue also is a fire, a world of evil among the parts of the body. It corrupts the whole body, sets the whole course of one's life on fire, and is itself set on fire by hell. All kinds of animals, birds, reptiles and sea creatures are being tamed and have been tamed by mankind, but no human being can tame the tongue. It is a restless evil, full of deadly poison. With the tongue we praise our Lord and Father, and with it we curse human beings, who have been made in God's likeness. Out of the same mouth come praise and cursing. My brothers and sisters, this should not be. Can both freshwater and saltwater flow from the same spring? My brothers and sisters, can a fig tree bear olives, or a grapevine bear figs? Neither can a salt spring produce fresh water.

What verses stood out to you in this passage from James?

What do you think James means when he says, "All kinds of animals, birds, reptiles and sea creatures are being tamed and have been tamed by mankind, but no human being can tame the tongue. It is a restless evil, full of deadly poison?"

If no human being can tame the tongue, then who can?

Reflect on the Holy Spirit and the impact the Holy Spirit has on your life. What steps can you take to help tame your tongue?

Now let's revisit our original question. What do you say on a daily, weekly, or monthly basis that you feel is offensive to God? Put a line through everything you just wrote that you say is offensive to God. Today, let's choose to no longer be this person. Today, we have beautiful tongues; let's make an oath with ourselves to move forward.

We do not want to give our adversary a foothold into our lives:

Do not give the devil a foothold. (Ephesians 4:27)

We are going to fail, but we will remember, today, that we have Jesus in our hearts. He will convict us when we say something offensive to God. We will then repent, let it go, breath out, and move on.

Don't ever let any sin hold you back from being a child of God. He designed you perfectly. You are unique, and you have a purpose—trust in this.

Don't let the sins of others keep you from having a relationship with Jesus Christ. People will sometimes let you down, and their sins will impact you in a negative way. When this happens, keep Jesus as your center. When you turn to him, he will guide you through. Always watch your tongue and be a light—even if no one around you is being a light.

Sweet sister, let your light shine bright for all to see. Hold tight to Jesus, his Word, and his values and morals—and always trust in him.

Jesus and Beelzebub

As you read Matthew 12:22–37, underline and/or highlight verses that stick out to you.

"Then they brought him a demon-possessed man who was blind and mute, and Jesus healed him, so that he could both talk and see. All the people were astonished and said, "Could this be the Son of David?" But when the Pharisees heard this, they said, "It is only by Beelzebub, the prince of demons, that this fellow drives out demons."

Jesus knew their thoughts and said to them, "Every kingdom divided against itself will be ruined, and every city or household divided against itself will not stand. If Satan drives out Satan, he is divided against himself. How then can his kingdom stand? And if I drive out demons by Beelzebub, by whom do your people drive them out? So then, they will be your judges. But if it is by the Spirit of God that I drive out demons, then the kingdom of God has come upon you." Or again, how can anyone enter a strong man's house and carry off his possessions unless he first ties up the strong man? Then he can plunder his house. Whoever is not with me is against me, and whoever does not gather with me scatters. And so I will tell you, every kind of sin and slander can be forgiven, but blasphemy against the Spirit will not be forgiven. Anyone who speaks a word against the Son of Man will be forgiven, but anyone who speaks against the Holy Spirit will not be forgiven, either in this age or in the age to come. Make a tree good and its fruit will be good or make a tree bad and its fruit will be bad, for a tree is recognized by its fruit. You brood of vipers, how can you who are evil say anything good? For the mouth speaks what the heart is full of. A good man brings good things out of the good stored up in him, and an evil man brings evil things out of the evil stored up in him. But I tell you that everyone will have to give account on the Day of Judgment for every empty word they have spoken. For by your words you will be acquitted, and by your words you will be condemned."

Reflection

- What verses from Matthew 12:22–37 impacted you the most?

- Do you realize your words are a reflection of who you are and what is inside your heart?

- Have you ever wondered, "How do others really see me?"

Go back to Matthew 12, read the verse that is underlined, and review it.

The Holy Spirit is the third person of the Trinity. God is spiritually active in the world. The Holy Spirit plays a vital part in our walks with Jesus. God is spiritually active in our lives. We learned from James that our tongues can't be tamed by human beings alone. It is imperative that we dig into the Spirit to help us with our words. It is impossible to tame our tongues on our own merit.

The book of Matthew taught us how Jesus says if anyone speaks against the Holy Spirit, it will not be forgiven. The Holy Spirit is the best gift we will ever receive in this lifetime. To truly tame our tongues, tame our words, and become more aware of when we gossip, we must embrace the Holy Spirit and draw near to his role in our lives. Every morning, we have to seek the Holy Spirit and say a quick prayer for him to cover our tongues so his fruits will flow out of our mouths:

> But the fruit of the Spirit is love, joy, peace, forbearance, kindness, goodness, faithfulness, gentleness, and self-control. Against such things there is no law. (Galatians 5:22)

As we close today, let's give ourselves some grace with our past and future words. Let's repent for any unwholesome words we have said in the past. Let's move forward and no longer be women who speak offensive or disrespectful words. If we fail along the way, it's okay. Don't give up. If we want to embrace the Holy Spirit daily, we can't do it alone.

You've got this, sister. This week, we are going to journal about our words, our characters, our tongues, and our actions. Invite the Holy Spirit into your journaling time. He is here to guide you, and he is spiritually active in your life.

As we close, let's personalize this verse from Ephesians 4:29 by inserting your name in the blank:

> Do not let any unwholesome talk come out of_____'s mouth, but only what is helpful for building others up according to their needs, that it may benefit those who listen.

Let's wrap up today's lesson with a prayer. Dig into the Spirit, sister. We can do this. Let's enter through the narrow gate together.

> Enter through the narrow gate. For wide is the gate and broad is the road that leads to destruction, and many enter through it. But small is the gate and narrow the road that leads to life, and only a few find it. (Matthew 7:13–14)

Personal Journal Time

- Based on how God sees you, what would it look like to present your character to the world?
- Do you want to be seen as an honest, loyal person? How else do you want to be seen?
- Reflect on the everyday words you use to communicate. Do you cuss? Do you say things that could be considered ungodly? Remember that your words are a reflection of who you are on the inside and what is inside your heart. Journal about this. Invite the Holy Spirit to help you.
- How are your actions when you are around big crowds of people or with friends? Are you always on your phone, playing video games, or texting? Are you open, ready to meet new friends, or spend quality time with the friends you are with? Are you living in the present?

Prayer

Dear Jesus,
Thank you for this command, for demanding respect from us. Thank you for being the ultimate example of how to require respect from others. Thank you for opening my eyes to see how badly it hurts you to take your name in vain and speak badly toward others. Please convict me when I am unaware of myself. Continue to open my eyes to see that what I say affects people. Let my voice and my words be a reflection of you. Please show me where I have hurt others and give me the courage to apologize and make it right. Let me be strong to not be a follower of this earth but a follower of you Lord. When others are lowering themselves to speak against you or others, give me your mighty strength to speak up or be quiet! Please, Lord, use my words to uplift, encourage, and show your love to others!
In your sweet name,
Amen

Nothing in all creation is hidden from God's sight. Everything is uncovered and laid bare before the eyes of him whom we must give account. (Hebrews 4:13)

❦ *Personal Journal Time: Session 3*

As you begin your journaling, remember to begin with a prayer. Invite the Holy Spirit in, refer to all the questions from this session to help guide you, become vulnerable, and add scriptures!

Questions for Guidance

- Based on how God sees you, what would it look like to present your character to the world?
- Do you want to be seen as an honest, loyal person? How else do you want to be seen?
- Reflect on the everyday words you use to communicate. Do you cuss? Do you say things that could be considered ungodly? Remember that your words are a reflection of who you are on the inside and what is inside your heart. Journal about this. Invite the Holy Spirit to help you.
- How are your actions when you are around big crowds of people or with friends? Are you always on your phone, playing video games, or texting? Are you open, ready to meet new friends, or spend quality time with the friends you are with? Are you living in the present?

Frankincense and Myrrh

Session

4

Commandment 4

Observe the Sabbath day by keeping it holy.
—Deuteronomy 5:12–15

Let's start today by reflecting and journaling about the following questions:

- When you think of a day of rest, what do you think?

- What am I resting from?

- Jesus says you are to rest from the world. What does this look like to you?

- What is the difference is between *earthly* rest and *heavenly* rest?

> Going on from that place, he went into their synagogue, and a man with
> a shriveled hand was there. Looking for a reason to bring charges against
> Jesus, they asked him, "Is it lawful to heal on the Sabbath?" He said to
> them, "If any of you has a sheep and it falls into a pit on the Sabbath, will
> you not take hold of it and lift it out? How much more valuable is a person
> than a sheep! Therefore it is lawful to do good on the Sabbath." Then he
> said to the man, "Stretch out your hand." So he stretched it out and it was
> completely restored, just as sound as the other. But the Pharisees went
> out and plotted how they might kill Jesus. (Matthew 12:9–14)

Remember—resting from the Sabbath doesn't mean you ignore a friend in need because
you are in a day of rest. You rest in the Lord, lean into him, and still lend a hand to
your loved ones.

> Keep this Book of the Law always on your lips; meditate on it day and
> night, so that you may be careful to do everything written in it. Then
> you will be prosperous and successful. (Joshua 1:8)

> Whoever believes in me, as the Scripture has said, streams of living water
> will flow from within him. (John 7:38)

How do we become more aware of the streams of living water that are flowing from within us (John 7:38)? By becoming biblically literate, by reading the Bible, and by studying it.

The Armor of God

In our lives, we sometimes live like disaster isn't going to hit us. We float through life—sometimes barely in God's Word—because everything is going well. What is the purpose of this? By not staying in God's Word daily, we are slowly taking off our armor. In the book of Ephesians, Paul talks about putting up the full armor of God:

> Finally, be strong in the Lord and in his mighty power. Put on the full armor of God, so that you can take your stand against the devil's schemes. For our struggle is not against flesh and blood, but against the rulers, against the authorities, against the powers of this dark world and against the spiritual forces of evil in the heavenly realms. Therefore put on the full armor of God, so that when the day of evil comes, you may be able to stand your ground, and after you have done everything, to stand.
>
> Stand firm them, with the belt of truth buckled around your waist, with the breastplate of righteousness in place, and with your feet fitted with the readiness that comes from the Gospel of peace. In addition to all this, take up the shield of faith, with which you can extinguish all the flaming arrows of the evil one. Take the helmet of salvation and the sword of the Spirit, which is the Word of God.
>
> And pray in the Spirit on all occasions with all kinds of prayers and requests. With this in mind, be alert and always keep on praying for all the Lord's people. (Ephesians 6:10–19)

The Blueprint Projects is a personal quest to dive deep into your heart and soul. God wants you to find your truth, your strength, your peace, and your light in him.

Let's unravel the layers of scripture in Ephesians 6.

The Belt of Truth

- What is your personal truth?
- What do you stand for?
- Is your truth complete belief in the Trinity or something else?

Ladies, as Christians, Jesus is our core. Our belts are not securely fastened when we follow the world more than we follow Jesus. When our truth and confidence come from worldly desires and not the love and teachings of Jesus Christ, it is impossible to stand firm against Satan's evil schemes.

The Breastplate of Righteousness

- What is the definition of righteousness?
- What are the antonyms of righteousness?
- What are you presently doing that does not align with Christ?
- Is there anything in your life that brings short-term joy but has caused long-term pain?
- Search deep inside your heart—are you feeling a tug that something in your life isn't right?
- How does God want you to act or present yourself?

God did not place commands, rules, and morals in your life to steal your joy. He placed them there to enhance your life and bring the heavenly peace that only comes from above.

This week, we challenge you to open your Bible, dig into it, and research what God says about your current situation or any questions you might have. This is not to condemn or point fingers; it is to help you break free from anything that is holding you back from becoming a woman after God's own heart.

The Shoes of Peace

- What are the antonyms of peace?

- Do any of these antonyms of peace describe parts of your life in your current state?

- What areas in your life can you feel Jesus's peace?

In every area of your life where you don't feel Jesus's peace, stop, pray, and invite Jesus in. Allow his peace to cover you.

The Helmet of Salvation

- What is the definition of salvation?

- Do you feel you are being continually delivered from sin? If not, why is that?

Salvation is a friendship, a bond, and a relationship with God. Belief in Christ brings freedom, but it is also important to become aware of our sins and repent.

In your relationship with Christ, Jesus can't do all the work. He is able to help, but we have a responsibility too. A true relationship is a two-way street, and your relationship with him will flourish if you build it with him.

This week, meditate on how you can work on your relationship with Jesus. How can you get to know him on a more personal level?

Always remember that you are a child of God—and never forget it:
Dear friends, now we are children of God. (1 John 3:2)

Read Colossians 3:2–3, write it down, and meditate on this verse.

The Shield of Faith

- What is the definition of faith?

- Is faith something we do?

- What does it mean to have faith in God? Make your answer personal.

> Take up the shield of faith, with which you can extinguish all the flaming arrows of the evil one. (Ephesians 6)

Satan disguises himself as an angel of light:

> For such people are false apostles, deceitful workers, masquerading as apostles of Christ. And no wonder, for Satan himself masquerades as an angel of light. (2 Corinthians 11:13–14)

Where in your life has Satan lied to you? Where has he made you think you are someone other than a child of God?

If we are not firm in the truths from the Bible and in God's Word daily, then these questions can be confusing.

Satan's goal is to cover us with a spirit of confusion. However, through the Word of God, we get clarity. When our minds are focused on Jesus, it gives us the power to extinguish the "flaming arrows of the evil one."

Now that we have learned this truth, what does it mean to raise your shield? Make your answer personal.

The Sword of the Spirit

- Do you call on the Holy Spirit daily to fill you and speak through you and for you?

- Do you invite the Holy Spirit into your life daily to guide you?

- Do you read your Bible regularly?

We challenge you to pray over the scriptures. Speak them out loud. Scripture is the sword that is waiting to be used to guide and protect us.

When we are not dedicating ourselves to God and getting to know him—his love, his kindness, his strength, his goodness, and his power—we are losing our armor. So, when disaster hits, our helmets are off, our shields are cracked, and we can't find our shoes. We are scrambling, searching, and begging God to empower us. Let's not allow this to happen. Let's make a promise today to stay in God's Word daily, find rest in him, pray for our futures, and take up the full armor of God. We want to be strong prophetesses: women who are called by God to fight for God and his people.

It's time to start resting from the world and start finding a day to rest in him, in his love, and in his goodness. God makes laws and commands to protect us; we need to take the time each day and each week to refuel.

As humans, we will experience many heartaches and challenges. If we do not fill our souls up with God's love and the truth of his Word, we will become depleted, depressed, and tired all the time. The Spirit of God will energize you and fill you with his joy in any circumstance.

Dissecting a Verse

> Where there is no revelation, people cast off restraint; but blessed is the one who heeds wisdom's instruction. (Proverbs 29:18)

Look up synonyms for the following words and jot down a few:

- revelation
- restraint
- heeds

Look up Proverbs 29:18 in a different version than NIV and write it below:
In your own words, what does this verse mean to you? Write it down.

As a young woman, it is critical to partner with God and create a vision for yourself and your life. Remember that this vision is between you and God alone. Like your BP, this is not to be shared. Seek into Jesus for your vision and protect your heart and vision from worldly influences. Don't listen to others; listen to your heart. God will put deep in your heart whom he has made you to be.

It is commanded that we take one day to rest each week.

We challenge you to use this day to celebrate, reflect, and set goals.

Celebrate

The gift of the Holy Spirit gives us a reason to celebrate every single day:

> For the Spirit God gave us does not make us timid, but gives us power, love, and self-discipline. (2 Timothy 1:7)

You, sweet sister, have a heavenly power that is ignited through your belief and love for Jesus Christ.

Have you ever felt like you have no hope? Have you ever felt like you were living in a state of fear? Have you ever felt like nothing you do from an earthly perspective will change your circumstance? During these moments, remember that God is good. He is with you even during times of despair:

> So do not fear, for I am with you; do not be dismayed, for I am your God. I will strengthen you and help you; I will uphold you with my righteous right hand. (Isaiah 41:10)

When we go through a time of hopelessness, we need to:

- love our God with all our hearts and all our souls
- stay fervent and disciplined in prayer
- celebrate our Lord
- repent of our sins
- follow God's commands
- soak in God's unending grace in our lives

Sometimes, when we are going through trials, we don't want to celebrate. We feel so helpless. However, to get through trials, we need to fight. Your Bible is your sword.

Even though your life may feel like it's crumbling, this is the time to pray. Even though your life may feel like it's crumbling, this is the time to see true light through Jesus and celebrate God. Even in a battle, we can find gladness and joy through Jesus.

Ladies, we can feel like we are in a war—or are constantly being hit with struggles, worldly desires, and sin—but let's still celebrate that we have God! We have no idea what tomorrow is going to bring. When we are going through battles, when we feel that our situations are hopeless, let's definitely take time to mourn. However, let's also celebrate that we have Jesus Christ—and because of his great love, through the Holy Spirit, we always get to fight.

Let's celebrate that we get the freedom to sit in God's truth, soak in his Word, and rest in him to fill us with the power to fight for him. Armor on, ladies!

Spend some time right now reflecting on your three biggest battles.

Once you have written them down, write down the things that are worth celebrating through these battles:

I keep my eyes always on the Lord. With him at my right hand, I will not be shaken. (Psalm 16:8)

Today and going forward, let's begin to celebrate all of our successes. In the future, when we hit a trial or are going through a battle, let's still find joy and gladness in Jesus Christ.

How beautiful it is to be loved by our King!

As we close, let's personalize this verse from Psalm 62:5–8 by inserting your name in the blanks:

Yes, _____'s soul finds rest in God; _____'s hope comes from him. Truly he is _____'s rock and _____'s salvation; he is _____'s fortress, I will not be shaken. _____'s salvation and _____ honor depend on God; he is my mighty rock, my refuge. Trust in him at all times, _____; pour out your heart to him, for God is our refuge.

Personal Journal Time

Journal and reflect on setting goals and creating a vision for your future.

Short-Term Goals

- Do you spend time each day in the Word and praying?
- Do you present yourself to the world in the ways you intend to?
- Do you feel the people in your world can see Jesus in your attitude, actions, and reactions? Are you celebrating his unending love in your life?
- Do you accomplish the goals you set for yourself? Where do you fall short? What are your challenges? How can you overcome them better?

Remember that your value and worth are not your worldly achievements and successes! You're a princess of the Almighty God. His plan for you on earth might not look like success to worldly people. If you feel like you are lost or have taken a wrong turn—if you are in the Word and praying—your detour is right where God wants you.

Long-Term Goals

Where do you see your life in three, five, and ten years? Create a timeline. Create a mission and a vision statement for your life and for your faith. How do you get there? Once you have set your mission, vision, and goals in place, hand them over to Jesus.

Your goal-setting and vision pages do not need to be completed in one week; it might be a section you continually go back too. Pray about it, rest in God, and think about what you see for your life.

Now is the time to make your faith your own and make your faith personal. Let Jesus enter your heart and let him lead you on this journey. Let's put on the full armor of God this week and create a vision for our lives so we can be a force and a powerful prophetess who is fighting against the schemes of the devil and having the courage and strength to stand for Jesus and walk in his way every single day. Have fun resting in God this week!

Prayer

Pray for your rest this week. Pray for your reflection time and journaling. Pray that God opens your eyes to see his vision for you. By digging into God's love, celebrating who he is, getting to know him on a deeper level, and resting in who he is, your door will start to open, your faith will start to unfold, and your faith will begin to take shape and become your own!

We are praying for you as you travel on this journey toward freedom.

❦ *Personal Journal Time: Session 4*

As you begin your journaling, remember to begin with a prayer. Invite the Holy Spirit in, refer to all the questions from this session to help guide you, become vulnerable, and add scriptures!

Questions for Guidance

Short-Term Goals

- Do you spend time each day in the Word and praying?
- Do you present yourself to the world in the ways you intend to?
- Do you feel the people in your world can see Jesus in your attitude, actions, and reactions? Are you celebrating his unending love in your life?
- Do you accomplish the goals you set for yourself? Where do you fall short? What are your challenges? How can you overcome them better?

Long-Term Goals

Where do you see your life in three, five, and ten years? Create a timeline. Create a mission and a vision statement for your life and for your faith. How do you get there? Once you have set your mission, vision, and goals in place, hand them over to Jesus.

Fig Tree

Session 5

Commandment 5

Honor your father and your mother.
—Deuteronomy 5:16

Honor is a word we often hear, a word of high regard, a word that makes us think of kings and queens and palaces. When we think of honor, we sometimes relate it to the word *love*, but it is different.

Session 2 showed us that love stems from giving and acts of respect, goodness, and peace to your loved ones. Honor is a bit different. Honor is defined as "to regard with high respect, admire, value, appreciate, cherish, and adore, to fulfill an obligation or keep an agreement with."

God commands us to honor our parents, and out of this honor, hopefully comes love. God knows that some people are hard to love, but showing them honor is a silent way to shine his light on them. It sets us apart. Holding us to a higher standard is a way to honor God and love ourselves.

Reflect

- Do you have someone in your life who is hard to love, but you still show them honor? List their names below. Reread through the definitions in the above paragraph to understand the difference.

- Think of those difficult people in your life: brothers, sisters, friends, parents, grandparents, teammates, or employers. What do you do when they are rude? Write down your thoughts.

While God calls us to honor our fathers and mothers, God did not intend for this command to allow any child or person to be mistreated:

> Children, obey your parents in the Lord, for this is right. Honor your father and mother—which is the first commandment with a promise—so that it may go well with you and that you may enjoy a long life on the earth. Fathers, do not provoke your children to anger, but bring them up in the discipline and instruction of the Lord. (Ephesians 6:1–4)

> Children obey your parents in everything, for this pleases the Lord. Fathers, do not embitter your children, or they will become discouraged. (Colossians 3:20–21)

The Greek translation of the word *honor* is "to value as you would a precious gem." The people in our lives who we honor, we are commanded to put them above ourselves and do it in love.

"Honor your father and mother" was written as a symbol of God's relationship with us. God created this world, and he used our biological parents to create our own lives here on earth. To walk like Jesus in this world, we are commanded to honor the people who gave us life. However, some parents can be burdensome, mean, and heavy on our hearts.

If we choose honor and respect in these situations—instead of hate and being stuck in an angry state of mind—our lives will be filled with godly joy and a peace that is not of this world. *Burdensome* in the Hebrew language means "heavy, weighty, or difficult." Throughout our lives, we will have parents, friends, loved ones who are difficult to be around, but when we choose to honor and respect first, our lives will be long—and we will break free from unnecessary pain and heartache.

Solomon wrote the book of Proverbs and he knew that choosing to turn away from extreme anger or rage will bring us to a place of peace, goodness, and love:

A gentle answer turns away wrath but a harsh word stirs up anger. (Proverbs 15:1)

Let all bitterness and wrath and anger and clamor and slander be put away from you, along with all malice. Be kind to one another, tenderhearted, forgiving one another, as God in Christ forgave you. (Ephesians 4:31–32)

Christ forgives me of my sins, and he forgives you. He gave his life so we can live in eternity. If Jesus can die for us, we can start walking in the steps of honoring and respecting our parents.

God added a promise to this commandment: the only promise offered. If we follow this command, he promises us a long life. This signifies the importance to God:

Honor your father and your mother, as the Lord your God has commanded you, so that you may live long and that it may go well with you in the land the Lord your God is giving you. (Deuteronomy 5:16)

This was how God demonstrated his deep love for his children: the Israelites. He blessed them with a promise of a long life and the beloved promised land.

We are to treat our parents with the utmost respect even if they are infuriating and difficult. Before we have children of our own, we can feel God's love for us through the eyes of a child. After we birth or adopt our own children, a whole new depth and meaning opens up to us because we can then truly understand endless love. In the love for our children, we can catch a small glimpse of how much God truly loves us.

The Fifth Commandment is not going to be easy for some of us; it might even make you mad. You might feel a sense of rage in your body. You may even be feeling it as you read these words. Please trust in God, your Creator, hold tight to these words, pray to Jesus, and try to begin peeling the layers back one by one.

This, then, is how you should pray:
"Our Father in heaven,
hallowed be your name (keep God's name holy, treated with reverence)
your kingdom come,
Your will be done,
On earth as it is in heaven.
Give us today our daily bread,
And forgive us our debts,
As we also have forgiven our debtors.
And lead us not into temptation,

But deliver us from evil.:
For if you forgive other people when they sin against you, your heavenly Father will also forgive you. But if you do not forgive others their sins, your Father will not forgive your sins." (Matthew 6:9–15)

Spend ten minutes in reflection on these questions:

- Write down how "the world" directs you to react when someone is rude or mean, is talking about you behind your back, or does something to intentionally cause harm to you?

- How do you instinctively react when someone cuts you off in your car or a parent and/or loved one challenges you?

- Are you quick to pass judgment and/or anger toward someone for their unkind actions? Are you naturally slow to anger, slow to speak, and slow to react in a positive light?

The Bible also commands us to honor our employers, leaders, and teachers. Yep, ladies, this includes political leaders, fellow believers, law enforcement, and nonbelievers. We are to honor everyone around us, especially those who are mean to us. How we treat others matters to God, and it should matter to you! It is a reflection of what is in your heart. Honoring others honors God.

Today, let's be in prayer about our words, our actions, and our reactions toward our loved ones, teachers, bosses, and strangers. The tongue is a powerful weapon, and with the Holy Spirit's guidance, we can tame our tongues—no one else can do it for us.

As we move into more reflection time, let's review a verse from the book of Romans. As we read, reflect on the power of our tongues:

> Do not repay anyone evil for evil. Be careful to do what is right in the eyes of everyone. If it is possible, as far as it depends on you, live at peace with everyone. Do not take revenge, my dear friends, but leave room for God's wrath, for it is written: "It is mine to avenge; I will repay," says the Lord: "If your enemy is hungry, feed them; if he is thirsty, give him something to drink. In doing this, you will heap burning coals on his head." Do not be overcome by evil, but overcome evil with good. (Romans 12:17–21)

Ladies, jot down and share a time when someone mistreated you and how you responded. We want 100 percent honesty. Our goal is not to shame anyone but to discuss behaviors in our lives that may not be biblical so we can get raw with God—and with each other—and move forward as a prophetess: a woman called by God.

Most people in our lives want to be good-willed human beings. We want to be respectful, loving, humble, obedient, and appreciative, but we live in a world where outside influences directly affect our hearts. When our emotions run high—or when our anxiety becomes heightened—we tend to react in unloving ways.

We must always remember two things. First, our feelings often lie to us, and second, there are two sides to every story. You never know what the other person is going through or has gone through to get to their current emotional state. This is why we have to dig into scripture about controlling our anger and showing honor to every person who comes into our lives.

Listening and Doing

> My dear brothers and sisters, take note of this: Everyone should be quick
> to listen, slow to speak and slow to become angry, because human anger
> does not produce the righteousness that God desires. (James 1:19)

> Those who consider themselves religious and yet do not keep a tight
> rein on their tongues deceive themselves, and their religion is worthless.
> Religion that our God our Father accepts as pure and faultless is this: to
> look after orphans and widows in their distress and to keep oneself from
> being polluted by the world. (James 1:26–27)

James's words are so true when he tells us to keep ourselves from being polluted by the world, in other words, guarding our hearts against corruption. As we are growing in our spiritual discipline, taming our anger, and honoring loved ones around us, we also need to learn boundaries by guarding against corruption from the godless world.

Honoring in this world does not mean we get taken advantage of just because we are trying to be good-willed human beings. Take up your armor (Ephesians 6), tackle your current situation with scripture and Jesus, and know it is perfectly acceptable to set healthy boundaries. To discern good from evil, it is imperative to learn about boundaries and godly wisdom.

For further study on boundaries and what they look like from a biblical standpoint, we highly recommend *Boundaries: When to say Yes, How to Say No to Take Control of Your Life* by Henry Cloud and John Townsend.

As we move forward into another passage in the Bible, close your eyes while we read the following scripture and really take some time to let the words sink in. Think about what Jesus is saying here. Think about how to stand up for yourself in a Christian way—and not in the way the world teaches you. It is okay to be stern. After all, Jesus was stern and direct.

Someone special once said, "The hardest people in your life to love are the ones who need it the most." This statement has proven to be true time and time again! From a heavenly perspective, our lives aren't really about us. They are about Jesus and all of the people he places in our path.

An Eye for an Eye

> You have heard that it was said, "Eye for an eye, and tooth for tooth." But
> I tell you, do not resist an evil person. If anyone slaps you on the right

cheek, turn to them the other cheek also. And if anyone wants to sue you and take your shirt, hand over your coat as well. (Matthew 5:38–40)

What does this scripture mean?

- In the first part of this passage, Jesus is enforcing that a criminal be punished with equal severity of the crime or offense committed.
- Turning the other cheek means not returning wrong for wrong. Most human's natural instinct is to respond with disrespect. When we have wronged someone, we expect to receive the same type of treatment. Responding to disrespect with love gets the other person's attention. It demonstrates what being a Christian means.
- Some scholars believe this was also a way for Jesus to communicate equality between the one showing authority and dominance over a person. During this time period, people "cleaned" themselves with their left hands, so the initial slap would have been done with the right hand. For the person to follow through with the invitation to slap them across the other (left) cheek, they would have to use their unclean hand, which they would not do. That would demonstrate to the offender that they were equals.

Gratitude is defined as the quality of being thankful, showing appreciation to a neighbor, and returning kindness. Honor is defined as fulfilling an obligation, keeping an agreement, or viewing with great respect. Sacrifice is defined as the act of giving something up, important or valued, for the sake of other considerations or surrendering.

Gratitude, honor, and sacrifice coexist and are all related. When we put them together, we are truly women for Jesus!

Who are you grateful for in your life? Who has sacrificed their own time and money to pour into you? Think about it from an earthly and a heavenly perspective? Up to this point in your life, who has shown you honor just because they love you? Who has taught you God's Word and then followed up by instilling wisdom in your life to help you learn right from wrong?

There is a difference between knowledge and wisdom. Knowledge is learning the scripture, memorizing verses, and sacrificing your time to master God's Word. Wisdom is taking the knowledge you have learned and being able to discern the difference between truth and lies and light and darkness. Wisdom is learning from your sacrifices, learning from your knowledge, and pouring out gratitude, love, and honor to your neighbors. You can have all the knowledge in the world, but as you begin your life as a young adult, it's imperative you dig into wisdom and learn to discern truth from falsehood.

We encourage you this week to write a thank-you card to someone you are grateful for. Who has shown you God's truth? Who has empowered you? Who has led you toward Jesus? Who is always on your side, rooting for you, loving you, and standing alongside you? We challenge you to write them a card this week, mail it to them if you have to, and express your gratitude for their impact in your life.

We also encourage you to journal a prayer of thanks to Jesus, thanking him for his walk in your life up until now. You can write anything to him. With your words and prayers, you are showing him honor. Keep this prayer in your BP and refer back to it when you need a reminder about all that God, Jesus, and the Holy Spirit have done in your life. Let's spend the rest of this week—and the rest of our lives—honoring God and our neighbors. When we do this, life will be so much sweeter.

By holding yourself to this standard of behavior, you are demonstrating Jesus's light on the people in your life. Just by showing others honor, you could be impacting their hearts, which could turn them toward Jesus: "Well done, good and faithful servant" (Matthew 25:23).

As we close, let's personalize two verses by inserting your name in the blanks:

> Let _____ give thanks to the Lord for his unfailing love and his wonderful deeds for humankind. Let _____ sacrifice, thank offerings, and tell of his works with songs of joy. (Psalm 107:21–22)

> Do not let any unwholesome talk come out of _____'s mouth, but only what is helpful for building others up according to their needs, that it may benefit those who listen. (Ephesians 4:29)

We are praying for you, sweet sister. God is so good.

Personal Journal Time

- Write a prayer of thanks to Jesus, thanking him for his walk in your life up until now. By your words and prayers, you are showing him honor. Continually go back to this journal page, celebrating his love for you and giving thanks to Jesus for your life.
- Based on this command and its teaching, set personal expectations for how you want to treat those who have authority over you: parents, grandparents, police, employers, etc. Write down scriptures to help you! Think about your character.

- What are your hot buttons in the heat of the moment? List them. Going forward, what will you do to be strong and have self-control? Look up and study scriptures to help you with this.

Challenge

Write a thank you card to someone. We challenge you to give this card to someone you are grateful for. Write in it, pray over it, and give to a person who has mentored you and/or helped you deepen your relationship with Jesus Christ.

Prayer

Each day, spend time praying and meditating on this prayer:

> Dear Jesus,
> Thank you for this command. Thank you for shining a light on all the places in my heart and soul where there is insecurity and hurt. Please heal me. Fill me with your confidence and peace. Please give me the wisdom and understanding I need to be honorable in conflicts going forward. Please convict my heart when I am not honorable. Please let me shine a light where there is darkness. Let them see you through my reactions and actions.
> In your heavenly name,
> Amen

❦ *Personal Journal Time: Session 5*

As you begin your journaling, remember to begin with a prayer. Invite the Holy Spirit in, refer to all the questions from this session to help guide you, become vulnerable, and add scriptures!

Questions for Guidance

- Write a prayer of thanks to Jesus, thanking him for his walk in your life up until now. By your words and prayers, you are showing him honor. Continually go back to this journal page, celebrating his love for you and giving thanks to Jesus for your life.
- Based on this command and its teaching, set personal expectations for how you want to treat those who have authority over you: parents, grandparents, police, employers, etc. Write down scriptures to help you! Think about your character.
- What are your hot buttons in the heat of the moment? List them. Going forward, what will you do to be strong and have self-control? Look up and study scriptures to help you with this.

Fig Branch

Session 6

Commandment 6

> You shall not murder.
> —Deuteronomy 5:17

Believe it or not, this command from God brings up controversy. Many people quote this commandment as saying, "Thou shall not kill," but the actual command is "Thou shall not murder." In the Hebrew language, there is a major difference between the acts of murder and the act of killing. The Hebrew word used for murder is "*ratsach,*" which translates to murder as an unlawful act.

One of the hardest parts to read in the Bible is when God kills or commands someone be killed. How can a God who loves us deeply kill or have anyone killed?

When God takes another life or commands someone in the Bible, it is lawful. When God takes a life in the Bible, that person was, or those persons were at war with God or had killed one of his people. When he commands men, women, and children to be killed or kills them, many scholars believe he is bringing the children to heaven out of the grasp of the evil one. He is showing the ultimate form of mercy to these babies by taking them out of the evil surrounding them. It is always lawful to kill in times of war, self-defense, or as punishment for taking another's life unlawfully.

The price for murder is steep:

> Whoever sheds humans blood, by humans shall their blood be shed; for in the image of God has God made mankind. (Genesis 9:6)

The consequence of sin is just as steep:

> If anyone strikes someone a fatal blow with an iron object, that person is a murderer, the murderer is to be put to death. Or if anyone is holding a stone and strikes someone a fatal blow with it, that person is a murderer, the murderer is to be put to death. (Numbers 35:16–17)

Through these verses, we learn how special we are to God. We are to be cherished and loved. Humankind is made in the image of God, and it is an unlawful act to murder. Oftentimes, followers of Christ are so troubled when a child dies or is killed. There are so many questions. Why? What happens to them? Let's have God's precepts answer all our questions and concerns:

- Read: 1 Corinthians 7:14
- Write: What part of this passage speaks to you?

- Read: 2 Samuel 12:15–23
- Write: What does this passage mean?

- Read: Isaiah 57:1
- Write: Whom does "the righteous" include?

- Read: Luke 18:15–17
- Write: What does "for the Kingdom of God belongs to such as these" mean?

One of the toughest issues we face when dealing with death is suicide. Is this an act of murder to a person's own body? When this happens to a loved one, how do we take steps towards healing?

Many of us know someone or have loved someone who has committed or will commit suicide. It's a growing epidemic in America and throughout the world. It is truly devastating. It haunts those of us affected. What happens to our loved ones who have perished? No one truly knows 100 percent God's views on this. Some people who have dedicated their lives studying the Bible have differing views on this subject.

As followers of Christ, it is true that God made no mistakes when creating you and your loved ones. He made each of us in his image. Maybe he didn't give us an answer for a reason. We know that God is pure love, his love for us never ends, and it never runs out. He is our Healer, our Protector, and our Redeemer.

If you are suffering from a loved one that has committed suicide or you personally have suicidal thoughts or had them, we are deeply praying for you. Please reach out to a loved one, a pastor, or a mentor to seek help and guidance. We recommend contacting the Suicide Prevention Lifeline, which is open twenty-four hours per day, at 1.800.273. TALK (8255).

Through scripture, we learn that we are never alone, we always have hope, and we were made for a purpose. God sent his Son, Jesus, to die for *all* sins.

Nothing can separate you or me from the love of God:

> For I am convinced that neither death nor life, neither angels nor demons, neither the present nor the future, nor any powers, neither height nor depth, nor anything else in all creation, will be able to separate us from the love of God that is in Christ Jesus our Lord. (Romans 8:38–39)

> "When you were dead in your sins and in the uncircumcision of your flesh, God made you alive with Christ. He forgave us all our sins, having canceled the charge of our legal indebtedness, which stood against us and

condemned us; he has taken it away, nailing it to the cross. (Colossians 2:13–14)

When we go before God with open hearts, giving him everything we have, he forgives us of our sins. Through Christ being nailed to the cross, we are forgiven:

> You will seek me and find me when you seek me with all your heart. (Jeremiah 29:13)

Ladies, seek Jesus with all your heart and soul. We believe God gave us this specific commandment because he loves us and wants to enhance our lives—and not destroy them. To God, it is insulting to take another person's life—and it is unlawful to do so because God created each and every one of us perfectly in his own image.

In our lifetimes, most of us will never be put in the position to actually murder another person, but how many times have you felt true anger, spite, or jealousy for someone else? Write down your thoughts.

An informal definition of murder is to punish severely or to be very angry with. Some synonyms of the verb murder are to thrash, blot out, knock off, destroy, abolish, or misuse. These words can directly relate to the act of anger.

Right now, let's transition from the term murder to *anger*. Apostle Paul wrote about anger in the book of Colossians:

Living as Those Made Alive in Christ

> Since, then, you have been raised with Christ, set your hearts on things above, where Christ is, seated at the right hand of God. Set your minds on things above, not on earthly things. For you died, and your life is now hidden with Christ in God. When Christ, who is your life, appears, then you also will appear with him in glory. Put to death, therefore, whatever belongs to your earthly nature: sexual immorality, impurity, lust, evil desires, and greed, which is idolatry. Because of these, the wrath

of God is coming. You used to walk in these ways, in the life you once lived. But now you must also rid yourselves of all such things as these: anger, rage, malice, slander, and filthy language from your lips. Do not lie to each other, since you have taken off your old self with its practices and have put on the new self, which is being renewed in knowledge in the image of its Creator. Here there is no Gentile or Jew, circumcised or uncircumcised, barbarian, Scythian, slave or free, but Christ is all, and is in all. Therefore, as God's chosen people, holy and dearly loved, clothe yourselves with compassion, kindness, humility, gentleness, and patience. Bear with each other and forgive one another if any of you has a grievance against someone. Forgive as the Lord forgave you. And over all these virtues put on love, which binds them all together in perfect unity. Let the peace of Christ rule in your hearts, since as members of one body you were called to peace. And be thankful. Let the message of Christ dwell among you richly as you teach and admonish one another with all wisdom through psalms, hymns, and songs from the Spirit, singing to God with gratitude in your hearts. And whatever you do, whether in word or deed, do it all in the name of the Lord Jesus, giving thanks to God the Father through him. (Colossians 3:1–17)

What stands out to you the most after reading this passage?

You have heard that it was said to the people long ago, "You shall not murder," and anyone who murders will be subject to judgment. But I tell you that anyone who is angry with a brother or sister will be subject to judgment. Again, anyone who says to a brother or sister, "Raca" (an Aramaic word for *contempt*) is answerable to the court. And anyone who says "You fool" will be in danger of the fire of hell. (Matthew 5:21–22)

Jesus and Paul teach us that we can't murder anyone—and we cannot be angry with our brothers and sisters. We must learn to forgive always, be even-tempered, and find strength, freedom, and self-control through Jesus Christ. How do we do this? How do we go through life without being angry with anyone? Let's learn.

We pray! We stand firm in our faith, we read our Bibles, we learn God's precepts, we put on our armor (Ephesians 6), and we find ourselves some great prayer partners!

> The fear of the Lord is the beginning of wisdom. And knowledge of the Holy One is understanding. (Proverbs 9:10)

We gain insight and wisdom by fearing the Lord and walking in his path. Through this, we gain the peace of God, which transcends all understanding and guards our hearts and minds in Christ Jesus (Philippians 4:7).

Heavenly peace will help us stay calm in times of earthly anger:

> Be alert and of sober mind. Your enemy the devil prowls around like a roaring lion looking for someone to devour. Resist him, standing firm in the faith, because you know that the family of believers throughout the world is undergoing the same kind of sufferings. (1 Peter 5:8–9)

Let's make it a point today to stop showing anger and rage to our loved ones and peers. We cannot let the enemy devour us; a roaring lion cannot devour us. How do we keep this from happening? We must connect with other sisters in Christ. We must come together, discuss the sufferings we have experienced, proclaim our praises, lift one another up in truth and light, and pray for each other.

Since we are wearing our armor today, let's review what the full armor of God looks like:

> Put on the full armor of God, so that you can take your stand against the devil's schemes. For our struggle is not against flesh and blood, but against the rulers, against the authorities, against the powers of this dark world and against the spiritual forces of evil in the heavenly realms. Therefore put on the full armor of God, so that when the day of evil comes, you may be able to stand your ground, and after you have done everything, to stand. Stand firm then, with the belt of truth buckled around your waist, with the breastplate of righteousness in place, and with your feet fitted with the readiness that comes from the Gospel of peace. In addition to all this, take up the shield of faith, with which you can extinguish all the flaming arrows of the evil one. (Ephesians 6:11–16)

In week 4 and 5, we discussed how important it is to take up the full armor of God by staying in the Word, keeping your (helmet) mind strong, acting on the Word, acting in faith, knowing God's truth is the only truth, and letting God's peace prevail.

The past weeks have been amazing, and Satan is most likely not happy about your interest in God and deepening your faith. Satan is never happy when you are on the right track. He is a grump! Satan is sneaky, but he is not too smart. His evil tactics become so easy to identify that they will make you giggle.

Sister, the thing that activates and keeps all the pieces of the armor connected, strong, and ready for battle against Satan is *prayer*!

One thing that is going to keep your anger under control is prayer. You must pray and ask God to protect you. With God's authority, command Satan to leave you and pray, pray, pray—and then continue to pray some more!

Let's dig into the power of prayer and its holiness. We must always pray and never give up:

> Then Jesus told his disciples a parable to show them that they should always pray and not give up. (Luke 18:1)

In the Old Testament, Moses knew the importance of the power of prayer. God chose Moses to deliver his chosen people, the Israelites, out of slavery in Egypt to the promised land.

Years before Jesus told this parable (Luke 18), Moses knew the power of prayer and never giving up. God spoke to Moses directly, and Moses knew how holy God's presence was. When Moses spent time with God, he set up a small structure, which resembled a shed, and called it his tent of meeting.

The Tent of Meeting

- Read: Exodus 33:7–11
- Write: What are your thoughts about Moses's tent of meeting? How could you incorporate this kind of structure into your life?

The power of prayer is extremely holy and going into the presence of God is a gift. As we continue to deepen our faith and begin to understand the importance of prayer, let's see if we can recreate a tent of meeting for ourselves. Let's create a prayer room in our bedroom with the door closed, in a closet, in a bathroom, or in an actual shed. We need a place where we can get alone with God to pray. We need a place to express our love for God and express our praises. We need a place that is quiet so we can hear the voice of God like Moses did many years ago.

> Then you will call on me and come and pray to me, and I will listen to you. You will seek me and find me when you seek me with all your heart. (Jeremiah 29:12–13)

God's Decree

Verse 12 is saying, "Yes, when you get serious about finding me and want it more than anything else, I'll make sure you won't be disappointed." Verse 13 is saying, "I'll turn things around for you. I'll bring you back from all the countries into which I drove you—bring you home to the place from which I sent you off into exile. You can count on it."

God is for you. He loves you and is always with you. When you go to God in prayer, He wants to deliver you from your sin, from your pain and trials. Go to him with an open heart (verse 13), so you can breathe in his presence, begin to heal, and begin to break free.

Deepening Your Prayer life

As we deepen our prayer lives and enter into the presence of God, we need to become aware about how holy and special it is to be in the presence of the Lord.

Let's study a few verses in the Old Testament and the New Testament about what was at stake for the price of our sins and for us to be able to enter into the presence of God.

> If anyone sins and does what is forbidden in any of the Lord's commands, even though they do not know it, they are guilty and will be held responsible. They are to bring to the priest as a guilt offering a ram from the flock, one without defect and of the proper value. In this way the priest will make atonement for them for the wrong they have committed unintentionally, and they will be forgiven. It is a guilt offering; they have been guilty of wrongdoing against the Lord. (Leviticus 5:17–19)

> Then Pilate took Jesus and had him flogged. The soldiers twisted together a crown of thorns and put it on his head. They clothed him in a purple robe and went up to him again and again, saying, "Hail, king of the Jews!" And they slapped him in the face. (John 19:1–3)

The definition of flogging is "to beat someone with a whip or stick as punishment or torture, to lash, to whip him or her so hard it tears their human flesh off their body." This is what happened to Jesus, and after his flogging, he had to carry his cross for miles on end to his crucifixion until death. He endured immense pain, immense agony, and immense grief so we could get the gift of the Holy Spirit. In his human body, he was sacrificing his body and blood for our sins.

In the Old Testament, to enter into the presence of God and receive forgiveness for their sins, they had to tear apart the skin of animals, kill them, and present them to God as an offering (Leviticus 5). In John 19, Jesus was delivered to be crucified. Jesus died so his Father could live in us, but his skin had to be torn apart and his body had to be mutilated and crucified to allow us the gift of God's presence.

We no longer have to offer animals for our sins because Jesus took the pain and suffering for us. That's how much he loves us. The presence of God is holy, special, and undeserved but because of Jesus's love, it's right here with us when we accept him as our Lord and Savior.

Going forward, the next time we take Communion and bow our heads in prayer, remember Jesus and his sacrifice and be reminded how holy the presence of God is and how rare and special this kind of agape love is. Hold tight to this as you begin your prayer journal.

Prayer Partner

As we close this week out, we would love to talk a bit about how important it is to find a prayer partner. Find a sister in Christ to turn to in times of need and praise. Find someone you are close with, who would love to stand alongside you, who supports you, and who is willing to continually pray for you.

This week, we challenge you to pray about a person in your life. Your prayer partner is someone you trust. Your prayer partner has a heart for Jesus. Ask God to open this door for you and remember that finding a prayer partner might not happen right away.

It can take deep prayer to find a trusting, loving prayer partner. Don't force anything. If you stay in constant prayer over this, God will provide. He always provides. His provision may not always be how we see it, but there is spiritual discipline to be learned while waiting on the Lord. Try not to get frustrated if situations are not changing or happening quickly because God has a plan for your life (Jeremiah 29:11).

Going forward, as you continue to grow your faith, a sister in Christ can help you fight against the schemes of the devil. You can be there for each other—in faith, in love, in times of joy and praise—and pray for each other every day.

For where two or three gather in my name, there am I with them. (Matthew 18:20)

This week, let's personalize Ephesians 6:11–16 (the armor of God) by inserting your name in the blanks:

_____, put on the full armor of God, so that you can take your stand against the devil's schemes. For _____, struggle is not against flesh and blood, but against the rulers, against the authorities, against the powers of this dark world, and against the spiritual forces of evil in the heavenly realms. Therefore, _____, put on the full armor of God, so that when the day of evil comes, you may be able to stand your ground, and after you have done everything, to stand. _____, stand firm then with the belt of truth buckled around your waist, with the breastplate of righteousness in place, and with your feet fitted with the readiness that comes from the Gospel of peace. In addition to all this, _____, take up the shield of faith, with which you can extinguish all the flaming arrows of the evil one.

Personal Journal Time

- Create your tent of meeting (your place of prayer).
- Create a prayer journal. Each day, take time to write out your prayers and praises. Pour your heart out to God. Nothing is off limits. God is a jealous God, and he wants you to need him desperately: all of your worries, insecurities, celebrations, wants, desires, and needs, all of it. He wants all of you. Write him every day as often as you can. Pray, pray, pray!
- Here's a challenge. Life is going to take you on a journey. Wherever you go, promise to take your prayer journal with you. Try to spend ten or fifteen minutes per day writing down your prayers, your worries, and your strongholds and hand them over to God daily. Write down your praises as well! This doesn't stop at the end of the week.
- The next challenge is to find a prayer partner. It should be someone you can trust and someone who also loves God. Try to commit to writing them your prayers once a day, once a week, or even once a month. As we begin making our faith our own, it's important to have others who love us and lift us up in prayer.

Prayer

Dear God,

We ask that you direct us in whom to trust to be our prayer partner. When led to a sister, please guide my heart to be a great support system for my prayer partner. Let me always keep her requests private and give me the wisdom to pray perfectly for her.

Please bless me with my own tent of meeting, my special place where I get to meet you, Lord, Jesus, and the Holy Spirit.

In this place, let me hear you and feel you—and open my heart, mind, and spirit to receive you completely.

Please let me never kill anyone with my words.

Let my words breathe life and love to everyone.

In your heavenly name,

Amen

✒ *Personal Journal Time: Session 6*

As you begin your journaling, remember to begin with a prayer. Invite the Holy Spirit in, refer to all the questions from this session to help guide you, become vulnerable, and add scriptures!

Questions for Guidance

- Create your tent of meeting (your place of prayer).
- Create a prayer journal. Each day, take time to write out your prayers and praises. Pour your heart out to God. Nothing is off limits. God is a jealous God, and he wants you to need him desperately: all of your worries, insecurities, celebrations, wants, desires, and needs, all of it. He wants all of you. Write him every day as often as you can. Pray, pray, pray!
- Life most likely already has and is going to take you on a journey. Wherever you go, we challenge you to take your prayer journal with you. Try to spend ten or fifteen minutes per day writing down your prayers, your worries, your strongholds and hand them over to God daily. Write down your praises as well! This doesn't stop at the end of this book.

Pomegranate

Session 7

Commandment 7

You shall not commit adultery.
—Deuteronomy 5:18

The day every little girl dreams about—the day you long for and smile just thinking about—is your wedding day. For most women, this is a day of glamour, makeup, and a beautiful white dress. You invite all your favorite people to share your joy, peace, goodness, kindness, and love.

Most girls dream about becoming a wife and eventually a mother, creating a legacy, and building a life with the man of your dreams. As fun as it is to dream about this special day, have you really thought about what kind of man you want to be holding hands with at the altar? What kind of man do you want to spend the rest of your life with? What characteristics do you want your husband to possess? A strong work ethic? Integrity? Faith? Will a man possessing all of these traits be attracted to you—or are there things within you that you need to tend to?

This week, we are going to discuss marriage and everything related to relationships, love, sexual impurity, and how to be the wife God designed you to be. The goal for this week is to see the difference between your wedding day and your marriage. We are going to start taking steps today to enter into a lasting marriage, a godly marriage, and a marriage with Jesus in the perfect center of it.

Before the "Perfect" Man

The desire to live happily ever after comes from the very essence of a young girl's biological makeup, it's embedded in our DNA. God created us to desire a handsome man to marry and have a family with. It might be kids, and might be fur babies. Some of you want to create the same life your parents did for you. Some of you are praying for something completely different. God knows the desires of your heart:

> Take delight in the Lord, and he will give you the desires of your heart.
> (Psalm 37:4)

> May he give you the desire of your heart and make all your plans succeed.
> (Psalm 20:4)

Sadly, some young ladies reading this have been victimized and don't feel worthy of this dream. Some feel it is impossible. Know that God will deal with the person or persons who violated you.

Some of you are impatient and won't be able to wait. Sweet sister, I pray that you hold strong. For all of you, this waiting period is a preparation period. This is your time to dig in and learn who you are in Christ so that you can have the blessing of the life God wants to give you. You are not a victim. You are deserving of the life of your dreams, but you need to strive to be whole before your Prince Charming joins you.

Scripture gives us three examples of women who had a desire for a family. Each woman chose their path, and each had a dramatic outcome.

Let's explore the marriage of Abraham and Sarah.

Read Genesis 16:1–6:

Note: At this point, Sarai was spelled with an I, which means "my princess."

- What did Sarai tell Abraham to do? (Genesis 16:2)

- What were some of the reasons Sarai took matters into her own hands?

- Do you think fear played a part in her decision?

- How did she feel about it after?

In verse 4, the Bible states Sarai looked "at contempt on her mistress."

In verse 5, Sarai is in an angry state because she believes Hagar looked at her with contempt as well on the day she conceived.

In Hebrew, contempt means "her mistress was dishonorable in her eyes" (verses 4 and 5).

In verse 2, Sarai told Abraham to perform this action. She took things into her own hands.

Contempt is defined as "a feeling that a person or a thing is beneath consideration, worthless, or deserving scorn." When we don't walk with God's plan for our lives, especially when it comes to dating, it can lead us down a path of feeling worthless, invaluable, or tossed around. We might feel like our existence doesn't matter and that we are easily replaceable.

We can learn some important things about the values of patience, kindness, gentleness, faithfulness, and self-control. These virtues are some of the fruits of the

Holy Spirit, and these virtues need to be embedded in our souls and in our hearts as we go through life.

Let's pray today that we bring God into all our situations, into our dating, and then into our marriages. Let's be a culture that leans on God for strength. I pray for patience, strength, and love—and then for more patience—as you wait for the Lord to open your path.

We can't let anxiety, impatience, or fear stand in the way. When we stand in God's love, we cast out all fear. Let's choose to wait on the Lord.

> There is no fear in love. But perfect love drives out fear, because fear has
> to do with punishment. The one who fears is not made perfect in love.
> (1 John 4:18)

When we decide to fear, we take matters into our own hands. When we try to fix things through what culture tells us, we will fall. If we fear, we won't be made perfect in love (1 John 4). When we act in fear, we fall—and we are giving Satan a foothold into our lives, which can create a stronghold that can last generations.

For Abraham and Sarai, their fall lasted thirteen years—and some people believe this fall has lasted for generations.

Abraham and Sarai lived in a state of confusion for thirteen years. Was Ishmael the heir of God's covenant? Was he going to be in the lineage of Jesus Christ? Was a child born out of fear going to be the beginning of God's covenant with his people? Let's read on to find out.

Isaac's Birth Promised: Read Genesis 17:15–21

When Abram and Hagar's son, Ishmael, was thirteen years old, God appeared to Abram and changed his name from Abram ("high father") to Abraham ("father of a multitude"). He changed Sarai's name ("my princess") to Sarah ("mother of nations").

- What did God tell Abraham (verse 1)?

- How did Abraham react (verse 2)?

- What are your initial thoughts about his reaction?

- Is there something in your life you have dreamed of for so long that you would laugh if God finally granted it to you?

As we reflect, remember that this type of reaction is common. We aren't here to point fingers; we are here to learn and grow in truth and knowledge.
Reads Genesis 21:1–21

- How old was Abraham when Isaac was born (verse 5)?

- What does Sarah do as a result of her jealousy and shame (verse 10)?

- What events in your life do you wish you could erase or send away? By sending an issue away, does it really make it go away?

Sarah was desperate for a baby. She was impatient with God's timing and offered her husband to her servant, Hagar. She did not wait on God to bless her with her baby. As a result of this sin, we still suffer the consequences of the fall.

Many scholars believe that Ishmael's descendants are the Arab/Muslim nation and that Isaac's descendants are the Jewish people. These two nations are still at war today.

How many times does fear take over us and cause us to make a wrong choice? Have you ever turned to the world to fix your situation? Have you ever looked for a quick fix instead of counting on God to step in? Are you being patient that his hand will guide you and strengthen you?

Jot down anything you learned from these passages in Genesis and can take with you in the years to come.

Hannah: Read 1 Samuel 1:1–20

In Hebrew, the name Hannah means favor or grace.

- What tugs on your heart the most from verses 3–9?

- Have you ever felt so distressed that you couldn't stop crying? Write a little about it.

- What did Hannah name her son and why (verse 20)?

Read 1 Samuel 1:24–28. Would you be able to give your son to God in such a way?

Children are a heritage from the Lord, offspring a reward from him. (Psalm 127:3)

Have you ever made a plea promise to God? If he would just _____, I will _____.

Read 1 Samuel 2:18–21 How many more children did God bless Hannah with?

What sex were Hannah's children (verse 21)?

Read 1 Samuel 3:19–21. What does this mean?

Hannah was obedient. She saw God as the only provider of her desperate desire for a baby. God needed Hannah to wait to birth her baby so he could be a prophet to Eli and minister to Israel at that specific time.

In biblical times, the significance of the firstborn was huge because the rights of the firstborn were not to be passed down to younger siblings. The firstborn were given double the inheritance and were favored by God and the family. God even required the firstborn animals to be sacrificed to him (first fruits).

It was not a coincidence that God needed Samuel to be Hannah's firstborn child.

He needed Samuel to be her first boy, especially because Eli's children were turning from God during this time. Samuel was positioned perfectly for his stewardship and was molding into God's perfect servant. Hannah, staying true to the meaning of her name, was given much favor and grace from God for her patience.

God's timing is perfect; he has a master plan. The book of Samuel is a spectacular story of how perfect God's timing truly is. He has a special job for every single person—including you!

If you are not married, this is your time to prepare yourself for your husband. Get out your prayer journals and ask God to shine a light on all the areas of your life he needs you to work on so you are ready for your husband when God brings him to you. This time of self-reflection should include deep prayer about what kind of man God truly wants for you. Spend time thinking about the questions we asked earlier. What kind of man do you want and need? Write prayers for your future husband. Pray over it. Ask God to speak to you and open your eyes and heart to his desire and then, sweet sister, write down what he whispers.

If you are married, this is the time to reflect on your marriage, open your prayer journal, let God in, open your heart to him, and allow him to shine a light on all the areas of your life that you need to work on to be the wife God destined you to be!

Mary and Joseph

This couple is well known by all humankind. They are famous for being Jesus's earthly parents. Jesus's mother was respected, loved, adored, cherished, and beautiful. Mary was a true prophetess. Joseph was strong, kind, patient, courageous, and handsome. He was a true warrior. Their relationship can teach us about relationships, commitment, love, and marriage.

Mary was about fourteen years old when Gabriel came to her, and she conceived Jesus through God. Mary was a devout Jewish girl who God specifically chose.

- She had to properly nurture herself and Jesus Christ for nine months.
- She had to raise Jesus until the appointed time when he would begin his ministry. Think about the responsibility of daily loving, caring for, and teaching the Savior. Think about the pressure to do it perfectly.
- She had to let him go! She trusted God like no mother has ever experienced. Her baby would be the ultimate sacrifice for all humanity.

The Birth of Jesus Foretold read Luke 1:26–56

One of the biggest takeaways from this chapter is Mary's character. Notice how prepared she was for her role. She was getting ready to be married, and then she was suddenly pregnant with the Savior of the world. She was facing a heartbreaking yet predestined life.

As a Jewish girl, she had memorized the first five books of the Old Testament. She knew the whole story. She knew the Messiah would come from a virgin. She knew he would somehow save all the people before her and all the people to come. She completely understood scripturally what Gabriel was saying to her. She was prepared in her character, the way she presented herself, her devotion and faith in God, and her heart. She was humble, and she didn't even know it. All of her was perfect to be the one and to be the Mother of Jesus.

Mary's Song of Praise: The Magnificat (Luke 1:46–55)

- How did Mary feel when Gabriel shared with her what was to happen?

- How did Mary respond?

We want to inspire you to become whole. We want to inspire you to become a devout woman who is called by God and prepared for anything that is thrown your way. To do this, you have to dig into the love of Jesus and work on yourself. You have to dig into the layers of who you really are and who you want to become. Be honest with yourself and invite God into your heart. Ignite the fire!

Utilize your prayer journal, write down everything you need to overcome, and truly pray for yourself. We challenge you to dig deep and work on exactly who God wants you to be.

Make note of Mary's Song of Praise: The Magnificat (Luke 1:46–55) and compare it to Hannah's song of prayer (1 Samuel 2:1–10). Study both songs of prayer and make a note of the similarities and differences. Hannah and Mary loved God with all their hearts and souls. They stayed faithful to God's commands, were extremely humble and gentle in spirit, and glorified God's strength. God found grace and favor in these beautiful women, and because of their humble spirit—instead of feeling entitled to their blessings—they proclaimed true, heartfelt thankfulness and love to God through a song of prayer.

When you turn your heart toward God, follow his commands, and love him with all your heart and soul, God will extend favor and grace to you as well. Turn to him, sweet sister, and never forget to be thankful for all the blessings in your life to come.

Joseph: read Matthew 1:18–25

- What did Joseph think about the situation before him?

- Could Mary have convinced Joseph that she was pregnant with Jesus?

Don't do God's job in your marriage. God's job is to work on your husband in all ways and mold him into his perfect servant. Stay out of God's way.

Joseph was chosen to be Jesus's earthly father. Joseph also knew the scriptures and was perfect for this role. We pray for each of you to pick a man who is ready for the role of being your husband. We also want to invite each of you to pray over your future husbands, future kids, and their spouses.

For all new brides, we recommend *The Beautiful Wife* by Sandy Ralya (www. beautifulwomanhood.com) as one of the best wedding presents you can get for yourself.

There is no perfect marriage. There is no perfect relationship. Jesus gives us a perfect picture of marriage through his relationship with the church. This "marriage" is only perfect because he is constantly bathing it with his own purification and constant forgiveness. He is mirroring his expectations of us in marriage. We are to love, forgive, and serve our spouses, especially when they don't deserve it. Give him the benefit of the doubt, accept him as he is, and remember your future husband will be doing the same for you.

We are not perfect either, and it will be just as hard for him to be married to you in the tough times.

> In a lawsuit the first to speak seems right, until someone comes forward
> and cross-examines. (Proverbs 18:17)

Ladies, there is only one perfect man: Jesus. It's easy to see others' faults and often hard to see our own. Look to yourself to grow and change throughout your life, especially in marriage and motherhood. When your future husband lets you down—and he will because he is human—know it is a blessing. God uses these times to grow and change our hearts and minds.

> Now for the matters you wrote about: "It is good for a man not to have sexual relations with a woman. But since sexual immorality is occurring, each man should have sexual relations with his own wife, and each woman with her own husband. The husband should fulfill his marital duty to his wife, and likewise the wife to her husband. The wife does not have authority over her own body but yields it to her husband. In the same way, the husband does not have authority over his own body but yields it to his wife. Do not deprive each other except perhaps by mutual consent and for a time, so that you may devote yourselves to prayer. Then come together again so that Satan will not tempt you because of your lack of self-control. I say this as a concession, not as a command. I wish that all of you were as I am. But each of you has your own gift from God; one has this gift, another has that." (1 Corinthians 7:1–7)

Adultery is an act that happens when your heart is not right with God, when you live a selfish life, and when you do not fear the Lord. People feel devastated when their partners cheat on them, they feel like it was a personal attack on them. Adultery is 100 percent selfish. The person committing the act is thinking of only themselves and not their partner. Why do we think living based on how we feel and what we like will bring us happiness and success? God will bring us success. God will bring us the fruits of life—and his way is always the better way.

This is a very valuable lesson for true success in marriage. Women often seek their happiness from men. Satan lies and tells us that men will make us feel valued, beautiful, important, and cherished. When our very human husbands can't fulfill all of this, we can cheat (and vice versa).

People cheat because they are literally looking for a human to fulfill what only Jesus can. Do the work to become whole in him, to 100 percent rely on him, and to fall in love with him! He will never let you down.

We need to be warriors for Christ. We need to cherish his word and live as though it means everything to us. We need to read scripture with other sisters in Christ, make it personable to our lives, and relate to it all the days of our lives.

Do you realize after the initial time you engage in sex, you are considered married? Therefore, each time you have sex with a different guy, you are taking that man as your husband. You are committing adultery with each new boyfriend:

> Do you not know that he who unites himself with a prostitute is one with her in body? For it is said, "The two will become one flesh." (1 Corinthians 6:16)
>
> He told her, Go, call your husband and come back. I have no husband, she replied. Jesus said to her, you are right when you say you have no husband. The fact is, you have had five husbands, and the man you now have is not your husband. What you have just said is quite true. (John 4:16–18)

Ladies, if you have asked Jesus into your heart, your body is his holy temple. Making the choice to have sex before marriage or have an affair with a married man or while married is one of the most devastating ways to defile God's holy temple, your precious body:

> Do you not know that your bodies are temples of the Holy Spirit, who is in you, whom you have received from God? You are not your own; you were bought at a price. Therefore, honor God with your bodies. (1 Corinthians 6:19–20)

The biggest blessing we have received from Jesus Christ is forgiveness. If you have already made a mistake, give yourself grace, love, and forgiveness. Jesus died for you on the cross; he will wash away all your sins. We live under the new law of grace. He will cleanse you as white as snow:

> "Come now, let us settle the matter," says the Lord. "Though your sins are like scarlet, they shall be as white as snow; though they are red as crimson, they shall be like wool." (Isaiah 1:18)

Always know there is absolutely nothing that has happened—or that you have done or will do—that can't be fixed through Jesus. He may require you to still suffer the consequence, but he will redeem you and your situation for his glory if you ask him to. Nothing is too big or too sinful for Jesus; he can use everything for good.

Journal about this because there will be a day when you need to desperately hear this over and over again.

This week, let's personalize 1 Corinthians 6:19–20 by inserting your name in the blanks:

> Do you not know, _____, that your body is a temple of the Holy Spirit, who is in you, whom you have received from God? You are not your own, _____; you were bought at a price. Therefore, _____, honor God with your body.

Personal Journal Time

- What traits do you want in your husband? What kind of man are you searching for? What are the three things that are necessary when searching for a partner to spend your life with?
- What kind of wife do you envision yourself as? What kind of love do you want to show your husband? What are three traits you want to possess?

Remember to dig into all the scripture we learned today to help guide you. Honesty is so important here because five or ten years down the road, when you are about to get married, you want to be able to look at your Blueprint and say, "Yes, this is the man I'm supposed to marry!" You may say, "Wow, this man is nothing like what I envisioned. He doesn't portray most of the godly characteristics Jesus wants for me in a husband."

Prayer

Dear God,
We lift ourselves up to you!

You say in Isaiah 1:18: "Though your sins are like scarlet, they shall be as white as snow; though they are as red as crimson, they shall be like wool." Thank you, God, for this gift of cleansing you give us.

We ask that as we move forward, you give us strength to resist the temptations of all the handsome boys who surround us. Open our eyes, our minds, and our hearts to discern the perfect characteristics of our future husbands. Give us the strength to wait for him!

Give us wisdom in our relationships to know if they are your will. Help us keep our eyes upon ourselves, our words, and our actions—and convict us when we are in the wrong.

Dear Lord, please mold us into who you want us to be!
In your name,
Amen

❦ *Personal Journal Time: Session 7*

As you begin your journaling, remember to begin with a prayer. Invite the Holy Spirit in, refer to all the questions from this session to help guide you, become vulnerable, and add scriptures!

Questions for Guidance

- What traits do you want in your husband? What kind of man are you searching for? What are the three things that are necessary when searching for a partner to spend your life with?
- What kind of wife do you envision yourself as? What kind of love do you want to show your husband? What are three traits you want to possess?

Lilies

Session 8

Commandment 8

You shall not steal.
—Deuteronomy 5:19

Put on the full armor of God, so that you can take your stand against the devil's schemes. (Ephesians 6:11)

This commandment touches on all the previous commandments. We challenge you, this week, to dig deep within yourself and be honest. By this time in our lives, we all should know we should not steal. It is wrong to take anything from another human being. Therefore, we will look at this commandment from a different perspective.

We will be learning, researching, reflecting, and writing where Satan has stolen a part of you based on each of the commandments we have discussed in the previous sessions.

Ladies, the Hebrew and Greek origin of the word *Satan* means adversary or accuser! *Adversary* is defined as one who contends with, opposes, or resists an enemy or opponent.

Similarly, adversary and advisory interconnect. Advisory is defined as having or consisting in the power to make recommendations but not to take action enforcing them, being in a position to consult, recommend, or provide advice or opinion. When someone advises, they influence your thinking, action, and direction.

Satan is always working to influence you and steer you away from God—just like he did with Eve—but he can't force you into anything. That is the free choice God gives us. Satan can just set up the playing field for you to fall directly into sin. He can make everything in your life feel like it's crumbling to make you turn you away from Jesus and enter into a life of sin. We can't let this happen. Armor on, ladies. We have to stay strong—just like Jesus stayed strong in Matthew 4:1–11.

Read Matthew 4:1–11, The Temptation of Jesus

Briefly discuss and/or journal about the following questions:

- How many days was Jesus fasting before he was tempted by Satan? Can you imagine how hungry he was? Have you ever gone more than twenty-four hours without food?

- How was Jesus tempted by the devil in this passage? In what three ways was Satan trying to steal pieces of Jesus?

- Why couldn't Satan force Jesus to do anything? Can you relate this to your own personal life? Explain.

Matthew teaches us how Satan can tempt us:

- food to fill our souls instead of the Word of God (Matthew 4:3)
- testing God to see if he really will come through. (Matthew 4:5)
- worshipping the values of the devil and things of this world to gain more riches (Matthew 4:9)

We cannot test God to see if he will come through. God always comes through, but it is in his perfect timing. He knows what is best for us, and we must trust in him. During this time of waiting, we can stay Holy by being patient, digging into the Word, learning the fruits of the Holy Spirit, and turning away from evil.

> He has made everything beautiful in its time. (Ecclesiastes 3:11)

> Trust in the Lord with all your heart, and do not lean on your own understanding. In all your ways acknowledge him, and he will make straight your paths. Be not wise in your own eyes: fear the Lord, and turn away from evil. It will be healing to your flesh and refreshment to your bones. (Proverbs 3:5–8)

Life will always be on God's timing. Satan can tempt us to choose earthly items—money, houses, cars, social media accounts, and material items—over God's love, but we shall only serve God and God alone. We have to carry this truth with us until the end of our days. We cannot covet or pick anything over God.

> Commit your way to the Lord; trust in him and he will do this: He will make your righteous reward shine like the dawn, your vindication like the noonday sun. Be still before the Lord and wait patiently for him; do not fret when people succeed in their ways, when they carry out their wicked schemes. (Psalm 37:5–7)

This does not mean God wants us to go without; when we get blessings in our lives, let's invite him into every area of it. This includes all our stuff, our relationships, our sex lives, and our social media accounts. Everything. We need to take care of the blessings God has trusted us with, respect our talents and gifts God has given us, accept all of them, and rely on Jesus as our one true identity.

Jesus Christ is perfect, and he never let Satan influence him to stray from his Father (Matthew 4:1–11). Ladies, we must stand strong because we are not perfect. We are broken. This week, we need to truly look in the mirror and realize how overwhelmed and shattered we are. We stray from God at times, we fall, and we make mistakes.

However, it is how we stand from those falls that truly matters. When we crash and burn, we must dig ourselves out of the pit and straight into the arms of Jesus.

His love for us never leaves; it is always the same. Hold tight to his blessings in your life.

Jesus Christ is the same yesterday and today and forever. (Hebrews 13:8)

Jesus was, will be, and is our perfect model, He is flawless and completely free from faults and defects. You and I, sister, are defected. We sometimes allow Satan to get his sneaky little fingers into our lives, and we begin to fall.

Let's stand strong together, united, in one body, one Holy Spirit residing in each of us. Let's continue to use Jesus as our ultimate example and turn to him when we are tested by our adversary.

Today, let's spend our time writing down where Satan steals from us and tempts us, focusing on the previous commandments we have studied.

Keep your Bible close by as you journal. Ask God to open your heart and mind to the scriptures he wants you to learn during this exercise. If you need help with scripture references, use the internet to search Bible verses or any Bible app you may have. Don't forget to pray!

I am the Lord your God; who brought you out of Egypt, out of the land of slavery. You shall have no other gods before me. (Deuteronomy 5:6–7)

Jesus replied: "Love the Lord your God with all your heart and with all your soul, and with all your mind. This is the first and greatest commandment. And the second is like it: 'Love your neighbor as yourself.' All the Law and Prophets hang on these two commandments" (Matthew 22:37–40)

God is helping you keep the focus on him. Don't steal his glory or let anyone else steal his glory. This separates you from God. Has Satan used you to steal his glory? Have you let someone close to you steal his glory? Where has Satan wiggled his way into your life in this area? Are you missing God's glory in your life? Are you turning to people and/or things other than him? Journal.

You shall not make for yourself an image in the form of anything in heaven above or on the earth beneath or in the waters below. (Deuteronomy 5:8)

Define *consumption*. What does consumption look like in your life? Do you think something—or someone—is unintentionally separating you from God and his love for you? By allowing yourself to become consumed with things like friends, boys, sports, phones, or anything else, you are not allowing yourself to stay on the path God has for you, separating you from God. Journal.

You shall not misuse the name of the Lord your God, for the Lord will not hold anyone guiltless who misuses his name. (Deuteronomy 5:11)

Taking the Lord's name in vain hurts God. Swearing and cursing robs you of a close relationship with God and your dignity. What is in your heart right now? What are you doing in your life to misuse the name of God? What are you doing well in this area? Journal.

Observe the Sabbath day by keeping it holy. (Deuteronomy 5:12)

By not taking this day to reconnect with God, recharge, and plan, you rob yourself of rejuvenation from God. Turning in the wrong direction can separate you from God. Are you finding heavenly rest? Are you finding rest through Jesus? What does earthly rest look like to you? It is not bad to take earthly rest, but how does it compare to heavenly rest? What is the difference? What steps can you take to start taking heavenly rest? Is Satan testing you in this area? Journal.

Honor your father and mother. (Deuteronomy 5:16)

Honoring your father and mother shows respect for you, your parents, and ultimately God. By not honoring them, you disrespect yourself and separate yourself from God. Think of all the elders in your life and list them: pastors, teachers, professors, parents, grandparents, friends, employees, and bosses. How can we show them more honor? How can we show more honor toward humanity?

Let your mind flow and write down everything that pops in your heart and mind. Journal.

Thou shall not murder. (Deuteronomy 5:17)

The most detestable action is to unlawfully take another's life. A person's life is literally stolen when they are murdered. This act completely separates you from God. Define anger. Now, define your own personal anger and what that looks like. Do you have anger brewing inside of you? Why? What can help relieve this anger? Where is Satan stealing your joy? How can you transition anger into Godly peace? Journal.

And the peace of God which transcends all understanding, will guard your hearts and minds in Christ Jesus. (Philippians 4:7)

Thou shall not commit adultery. (Deuteronomy 5:18)

If you cheat on your husband or steal another woman's husband, you rob yourself of self-respect, self-worth, dignity, and humility. You separate yourself from God. Have you ever cheated on your boyfriend? Have you ever cheated on a friend? Have you ever cheated your way through something? How did it make you feel? Cheating, in any shape or form, separates you from God. Jesus can always bring you back home, but we have to work on our hearts in this section.

Be honest with yourself, write it down, repent, turn back toward God, and move forward. You are a disciple for Jesus. You are loved by God. Don't let anything keep you chained to Satan and separated from God. You must break free. Pray. Journal.

Therefore, confess your sins to each other and pray for each other so that you may be healed. The prayer of a righteous person is powerful and effective. (James 5:16)

What does this verse mean?

All of the previous commands were made to protect us from Satan and keep us close to God. Don't let Satan wiggle his way into your life and steal your future and purpose while you are here on earth. God blesses us with the knowledge of how to fight Satan with the full armor (Ephesians 6).

No matter how happy, simple, or blessed your life is at the moment, keep the armor securely in place. When your defenses are down, Satan is creeping in.

> In your anger do not sin. Do not let the sun go down while you are still angry, and do not give the devil a foothold. Anyone who has been stealing must steal no longer, but must work, doing something useful with their own hands, that they may have something to share with those in need. (Ephesians 4:26–28)

Let's dig into this story with Jesus.

> Jesus used this figure of speech, but the Pharisees did not understand what he was telling them. Therefore, Jesus said again, "Very truly I tell you, I am the gate for the sheep. All who have come before me are thieves and robbers, but the sheep have not listened to them. I am the gate; whoever enters through me will be saved. They will come in and go out, and find pasture. The thief comes only to steal and kill and destroy; I have come that they may have life, and have it to the full." (John 10:6–10)

One of the most tragic ways Satan steals a person's life from God is through anxiety, depression, and even suicide. Feelings of anxiety are normal. It's God's way of heightening our awareness and bringing our attention into focus. Sadness is normal, but when our armor isn't fully intact, Satan will shower us with events and situations that compound the emotions of sadness and anxiety. Before we know it, we can be in a deep, dark pit. The only way out of the pit is a heavenly rope held by Jesus:

> The Jews who were there gathered around him, saying, "How long will you keep us in suspense? If you are the Messiah, tell us plainly." Jesus answered, "I did tell you, but you do not believe. The works I do in my Father's name testify about me, but you do not believe because you are not my sheep. My sheep listen to my voice; I know them, and they follow me. I give them eternal life, and they shall never perish; no one will snatch them out of my hand. My Father, who has given them to me, is greater than all; no one can snatch them out of my Father's hand. I and the Father are one." (John 10:24–30)

This week, let's personalize John 3:16–17 by inserting your name in the blanks:

> For God so loved _____ that he gave his one and only Son, that whoever believes in him shall not perish but have eternal life. For God did not send his Son into the world to condemn _____, but to save _____ through him.

Personal Journal Time

- Are there times when you feel yourself doing something that doesn't align with your values? How has digging into God's Word changed your action toward this?
- Name three people who you feel have an influence on you and why? Are they earthly or godly? Do they speak truth, knowledge, and godly wisdom? This journal question is not meant to have you take a person out of your life because they are not godly. The goal is to become aware of which truths are spilling into your heart and soul on a daily basis.
- In what area of your life do you feel insecure? Be honest. Pray and give your insecurities over to Jesus.
- What actions are you going to put in place to keep yourself strong against Satan's temptations and attacks?

The Ten Commandments are a mirror for our lives; they are given to us as rules to follow so we can live beautiful lives. God knows our struggles here on earth; he already knows we are going to fail at times. Doing this project today—and being honest and vulnerable with ourselves—will help us immediately recognize our plan of attack.

Then, in the future, if or when we fail, we are strong, we have a plan, and with the help of the Spirit, we can fight against this awful thief.

> Do not merely listen to the word, and so deceive yourselves. Do what it says. Anyone who listens to the word but does not do what it says is like someone who looks at his face in a mirror and, after looking at himself, goes away and immediately forgets what he looks like. But whoever looks intently into the perfect law that gives freedom, and continues in it—not forgetting what they have heard, but doing it—they will be blessed in what they do. (James 1:22–25)

Prayer

> Dear God,
>   We ask that you shine a bright light on anything that is stealing us from you. Give us the courage to set boundaries, break habits, step away from comforts, and end relationships so that we can be free of the wedge Satan has between us. With the authority of Jesus, we command Satan and his servants to leave every part of our lives. We invite the Holy Spirit into every crevice. We thank you for your truth God!
>   In your heavenly name,
> Amen

The thief comes only to steal and kill and destroy. I came that they may have life and have it abundantly. (John 10:10)

🖋 *Personal Journal Time: Session 8*

As you begin your journaling, remember to begin with a prayer. Invite the Holy Spirit in, refer to all the questions from this session to help guide you, become vulnerable, and add scriptures!

Questions for Guidance

- Are there times when you feel yourself doing something that doesn't align with your values? How has digging into God's Word changed your action toward this?
- Name three people who you feel have an influence on you and why? Are they earthly or godly? Do they speak truth, knowledge, and godly wisdom? This journal question is not meant to have you take a person out of your life because they are not godly. The goal is to become aware of which truths are spilling into your heart and soul on a daily basis.
- In what area of your life do you feel insecure? Be honest. Pray and give your insecurities over to Jesus.
- What actions are you going to put in place to keep yourself strong against Satan's temptations and attacks?

Olive Branch

Session 9

Commandment 9

You shall not give false testimony against your neighbor.
—Deuteronomy 5:20

As we begin this session, let's research what bear false witness truly means. Please look up the definition of bear false witness and its synonyms. Jot it down.

> There are six things the Lord hates, seven that are detestable to him:
> haughty (arrogant) eyes, a lying tongue, hands that shed innocent blood,
> a heart that devises wicked schemes, feet that are quick to rush into evil,
> a false witness who pours out lies and a person who stirs up conflict in
> the community. (Proverbs 6:16–19)

Today, we are shaping our hearts and discussing how we treat others, what we say about them, and how we present our truths to the world. Together, let's build our hearts for good and for kingdom work.

Reflection

What did God mean when he said *neighbor*?

Do you think God meant for your biggest enemy to be considered your neighbor?

> But to you who are listening I say: Love your enemies, do good to those who hate you, bless those who curse you, pray for those who mistreat you. If someone slaps you on one cheek, turn to them the other also. If someone takes your coat, do not withhold your shirt from them. Give to everyone who asks you, and if anyone takes what belongs to you, do not demand it back. Do to others as you would have them do to you.
>
> If you love those who love you, what credit is that to you? Even sinners love those who love them. And if you do good to those who are good to you, what credit is that to you? Even sinners do that. And if you lend to those from whom you expect repayment, what credit is that to you? Even sinners lend to sinners, expecting to be repaid in full. But love your enemies, do good to them, and lend to them without expecting to get anything back. Then your reward will be great, and you will be children of the Most High, because he is kind to the ungrateful and wicked. Be merciful, just as your Father is merciful. (Luke 6:27–36)

Jesus makes his expectations of us very clear. Does it make you squirm? It doesn't feel natural to be kind when someone is being cruel to you, does it? What about when you know someone is talking about you behind your back.

Think about times when someone has gossiped about you. How violated and vulnerable did you feel?

Think about a time when someone betrayed a confidence of yours. Did you know that it is a commandment to not lie about our neighbors? Did you know it is sinful to gossip—even if what you are saying is true.

Jots down your thoughts based on the above questions.

> You have heard that it was said to the people long ago, "You shall not murder, and anyone who murders will be subject to judgment." But I tell you that anyone who is angry with a brother or sister will be subject to judgment. Again, anyone who says to a brother or sister, "Raca," is answerable to the court. And anyone who says, "You fool!" will be in danger of the fire of hell. (Matthew 5:21–22)

This passage teaches us that words kill. Doesn't that sound pretty intense? According to the teachings of Jesus, the tongue has the power to kill another person, kill their heart, and kill their spirit. Gossiping, bullying, or talking behind someone's back can damage them for the rest of their life.

This week, the goal is to grasp the power of the tongue and the power of words. We may never be put in the position to kill another person, but we are put in a position to destroy another person from our words. The power of the female tongue can cause another person to suffer greatly. Their self-confidence, hearts, and souls can be crushed by our words result in anorexia, identity issues, cutting, or even suicide.

Our words can also crush a man's soul very easily. What we say, what we do, what we stand for, and how we act matters. As we are growing in our faith, it's time to understand how we can start to tame our tongues. It's imperative to begin breathing words from the Holy Spirit today. We can't do this alone; we need constant fellowship, sisters in Christ to stand alongside us, and most importantly, prayer.

Reflection Time

- Think of a time when someone talked behind your back or said something to you that you can remember vividly but it impacted you negatively?

- Now, think of a time when you have gossiped, talked behind someone's back, or cut them down. This may have been just a small thing, but what possible impact could it have on your neighbor? Write down your thoughts. You don't have to be specific here or write down names or exact situations. This isn't to shame anyone; it is merely to get us thinking.

- Write an example of a time when you felt hostile toward another person. Think about how you felt inside, how did your spirit feel? Journal.

- Think of a time you confided in a friend over a situation, but it turned into a gossip fest, putting someone else down to make you feel a tiny bit better. You don't have to say names here—just mention what happened and how it made you feel.

- Gossiping, even though wrong, can make you feel better from an earthly perspective, but is it right? Write down your thoughts.

We are working on our humility here. It is okay to confide in a prayer partner or a sister in Christ to work through issues, but it's not okay to gossip or talk badly about another person out of jealousy or rage.

As your relationship in Jesus grows, gossiping will feel less comforting. The Holy Spirit will start to convict your heart. If your stomach starts turning about the conversation you are in, shut it down. The tongue is a powerful weapon, and it has the ability to destroy people. Let's learn how to consistently pray to God to use our tongues for his glory and not our own.

John 15:9-19, The World Hates the Disciples

As the Father has loved me, so have I loved you. Now remain in my love. If you keep my commands, you will remain in my love, just as I have kept my Father's commands and remain in his love. I have told you this so that my joy may be in you and that your joy may be complete. My command is this: Love each other as I have loved you. Greater love has no one than this: to lay down one's life for one's friends. You are my friends if you do what I command. I no longer call you servants, because a servant does not know his master's business. Instead, I have called you friends, for everything that I learned from my Father I have made known to you. You did not choose me, but I chose you and appointed you so that you might go and bear fruit—fruit that will last—and so that whatever you ask in my name the Father will give you. This is my command: Love each other. If the world hates you, keep in mind that it hated me first. If you belonged to the world, it would love you as its own. As it is, you do not belong to the world, but I have chosen you out of the world. That is why the world hates you.

God chose you. Jesus calls us to be his disciples, to be his light here on earth, and to walk with the Spirit in our hearts so we can be Jesus's hands and feet. There will be times in your life when you must stand against culture or stand against evil. In the right situation, it is appropriate to be stern. There are times when you should stand up for yourself or others who cannot. If you hear friends or peers speaking poorly about another person, assess the situation and say a quick prayer to see how you should proceed. There will be times when the Holy Spirit nudges you to stand up for our brothers and sisters in need and not just turn a cold shoulder.

> This is how we know what love is: Jesus Christ laid down his life for us. And we ought to lay down our lives for our brothers and sisters. If anyone has material possessions and sees a brother or sister in need but has no pity on them, how can the love of God be in that person? (1 John 3:16–17)

We must align our lives with the truth from God's Word so we have the power to be disciples—even when culture is swaying us to act in a wrong way. Satan, the evil one, the adversary, loves a passive Christian.

Merriam-Webster defines *passive* as "open to outside impressions or influences, lacking in energy or will, lethargic, tending to not take an active or dominant part, existing or occurring without being active, open or direct."

Ladies, as you begin the process of making your faith your own, gaining independence, and gaining more responsibility, you cannot become passive. You cannot afford to become lethargic or lacking in energy or will when it comes to God, Jesus, and the Holy Spirit.

We cannot stress how important it is to make Jesus a dominant part of your life. Find the time to read your Bible, update your own personal Blueprint when necessary, find a church you love, and surround yourself with quality people. There will be times when you struggle, and there will be times when activities or a career will consume all your time. If you don't give God the time he wants and deserves, you will get burned out very quickly. The world can only give you earthly energy, which doesn't last very long before you feel burned out again and need to refuel. During this time, you will start to forget some of your truths, which leaves an open door for Satan to enter.

When we are tired, exhausted, or worn out, our tongues can start moving in the wrong direction. We start saying things we don't mean, and we start hurting people with our words. Remember to always find time to get your strength, your rejuvenation, and your comfort from God. God is the only one who can give you energy from above. Heavenly energy is unending energy. We need heavenly energy so our words, actions, and tongues can stay pure and loving—a direct resemblance of Jesus.

Wherever life takes us, let's constantly be a light. The deeper your relationship with God becomes, the more suffering you will most likely endure. Expect trials and tribulations. Suffering is just the way of life. We were born into sin. We were born into a wrecked world. Take heart. Jesus, our Lord and Savior, has conquered the world. Rejoice in him and know his truth is the only way of life. Follow it, demand it, and find peace in it. Rejoice that you are a child of God:

> For our struggle is not against flesh and blood, but against the rulers, against the authorities, against the powers of this dark world and against the spiritual forces of evil in the heavenly realms. (Ephesians 6:12)

> I have told you these things, so that in me you may have peace. In this world you will have trouble. But take heart! I have overcome the world. (John 16:33)

Jesus has overcome the world. He is for us, and we find our worth and value in him. Hold tight to this truth as you begin to journal this week.

This week, let's personalize Luke 6:45 by inserting your name in the blank:

> _____ brings good things out of the good stored up in her heart, and an evil woman brings evil things out of the evil stored up in her heart. For the mouth speaks what the heart is full of.

Personal Journal Time

How can you remove yourself when put in a situation that is turning toward gossip? After everything you have learned this week, how will you present yourself as a

Christian woman in this world? Take some time to write down new expectations, new behaviors, be in prayer, and let scripture help guide your plan.

Prayer

Dear Jesus,
Please from this day forward give us the confidence, strength, and humility to stop gossiping. Let us walk away from conversations that are not uplifting and encouraging.

Let us always tell the facts of an event and never embellish or hold the truth. Let us be brave to face consequences we don't want when we make mistakes. Take the temptation from us to cover for ourselves or others or falsely blame anyone else.

Give us your wisdom in the perfect way to stand up for others and ourselves in a way that shines a light on you and sets us apart.

Let us always be bold enough to represent you and not the world.

Dear Jesus, we thank you for this knowledge and wisdom!

In your name,

Amen

🕯 *Personal Journal Time: Session 9*

As you begin your journaling, remember to begin with a prayer. Invite the Holy Spirit in, refer to all the questions from this session to help guide you, become vulnerable, and add scriptures!

Questions for Guidance

How can you remove yourself when put in a situation that is turning toward gossip? After everything you have learned this week, how will you present yourself as a Christian woman in this world? Take some time to write down new expectations, new behaviors, be in prayer, and let scripture help guide your plan.

Session 10

Commandment 10

You shall not covet your neighbor's wife. You shall not set your
desire on your neighbor's house or land, his male or female servant,
his ox or donkey or anything that belongs to your neighbor.
—Deuteronomy 5:21

Let's begin by searching for the definition and synonyms for the word *covet*. Jot it down.

All throughout life's journey, we will have the worldly pressure to measure up. Our lives are always wondering, and this cultural pressure isn't going to let up. Is your hair amazing today? Are your lashes long? Is your style current? Is your college or career good enough? Jot down some cultural pressures you struggle with.

As you grow, these things evolve and change, but the comparison aspect stays the same. God desires us to be secure in whom he made us. He put careful thought and consideration into creating every little cell in your body and beautiful hair on your head.

Read Psalm 139, Search Me, O God, and Know My Heart

As you read, make note of any verses that stick out to you. When you read God's Holy Bible, it becomes alive. Some verses have the tendency to pop right off the page and fall into your heart. When this happens, we believe it is a nudge from the Holy Spirit.

Take note of these verses in Psalm 139, you were made for a purpose:

> For you created my inmost being; you knit me together in my mother's womb. I praise you because I am fearfully and wonderfully made; your works are wonderful, I know that full well.
> My frame was not hidden from you when I was made in the secret place, when I was woven together in the depths of the earth. Your eyes saw my uniformed body; all the days ordained for me were written in your book before one of them came to be. (Psalm 139:13–16)

In the five to six weeks from the time of conception to when the egg implants into the mother, you were truly God's secret. During that time, only he knew you existed. You were his secret treasure. From the time you were planted in your mother's womb, God was with you—and he is with you now and is forever shining his beautiful truth and light into your life. There is nowhere you can go, that he is not there. Even darkness is not dark to God; the night is bright as the day. If you experience any form of darkness, it turns to light with God by your side (Psalm 139:12)

To *covet* means to yearn to possess or have something; the need to compare stems from this. Comparison has the ability to destroy our hearts, desires, and God's plan for our lives.

If you are in a group setting, let's complete the self-esteem activity that deals with comparison (see appendix 1). If you are reading through this project on your own, please note that everyone shares the same insecurities. You are not alone. The self-esteem quiz demonstrates that we all share insecurity!

At the root of envy is comparison. Comparison is Satan's tool to make you feel less than, not smart enough, not pretty enough, not skinny enough, and not successful enough. Satan wants nothing more than to steal your joy and self-confidence so that you are crippled and unable to do what God has designed specifically for you. This is how he influences your behavior.

When we begin to focus on something we love and want what someone else has, it takes up a lot of real estate in our minds. We think, dream, and imagine. God is not shy to say bluntly that he is a jealous God. He doesn't want you to think about what you want. He wants you to be thanking him for what you have. Focus on him.

> Each one should test their own actions. Then they can take pride in themselves alone, without comparing themselves to someone else, for each one should carry their own load. (Galatians 6:4–5)

> But if you harbor bitter envy and selfish ambition in your hearts, do not boast about it or deny the truth. Such "wisdom" does not come down from heaven but is earthly, unspiritual, demonic. For where you have envy and selfish ambition, there you find disorder and every evil practice. (James 3:14–16)

God also created this command to protect us from violating other commandments. If you want an object or a thing too desperately, it may cause you to steal. If you covet another woman's husband or boyfriend, it could cause you to commit adultery. All of these acts force you to lie. We discussed this in week 8. Satan will 100 percent spend your lifetime trying to steal you away from God. He is working tirelessly to keep you from all of the magnificent things God has planned for you. Ironic, isn't it? We spend so much of our lives feeling unworthy, self-conscious, ugly, and unloved—just like Satan wants us to feel.

Think about how truly valuable you must be for Satan to spend his time working so hard to lure you away from God. All of God's commands are to protect us and keep us close to him.

One of Satan's biggest tools is to demoralize and plague us with the comparison flu through social media. Social media can be a blessing, but it can be a huge curse! The blessing is keeping in touch with friends and family near and far and creating a network of friendships and family. It can be used for business—and even promoting Christianity.

The curse of it is that our culture preys on the original sin of women, thinking they deserve and want more than they have or are given. It is a master of demeaning us, while creating insecurities in us and robbing us of our God-given individuality. All social media platforms use women and their posts to attract likes (traffic), and they profit from it.

Let's examine our hearts right now.

- How many times have you posted something R-rated on social media or compromised your integrity to get noticed and/or attention?
- How many secret social media accounts do you have?
- Even though this seems normal from an earthly perspective, how do you feel about it?

Study this verse and jot down your thought:

Test me, Lord, and try me, examine my heart and my mind. (Psalm 26:2)

God is everywhere; anything done in secret is a way for Satan to wiggle into your life. Satan loves secrets. How can you let your light truly shine if some of your life is hidden in secrecy and darkness? When we cover ourselves in God's Word and God's truth, it is a way of being with him and a way for God to examine our own hearts. What a blessing it is we have this beautiful book of true life!

Therefore, confess your sins to each other, and pray for each other so that you may be healed. (James 5:16)

For the love of money is the root of all kinds of evil. Some people, eager for money, have wandered from the faith and pierced themselves with many griefs. (1 Timothy 6:10)

Let's get real and be honest. Most of the time, social media uses people and their posts to make money. Our culture is dictating the popularity of those posts, and right now, our culture is stripping women of their self-respect, integrity, dignity, and self-worth. The world constantly tempts us to present ourselves on social media in a worldly way.

Social media can be used as a way to falsely build our self-esteem and self-worth. That feeling of validation you're craving is fleeting. Social media is literally a form of instant gratification. You get that feeling of approval, acceptance, and love. When it's gone, you crave more.

If you lean into Jesus to fulfill this need, the feeling he gives you when you seek him and pray isn't fleeting. It lasts. All of the ways you feel imperfect, all the things you hate, Jesus loves about you! He had a reason for creating you that specific, amazing way. Spend time with him about it and listen. He will help you appreciate all the things about yourself that you don't like. He will give you understanding about yourself if you ask.

Ladies, we must lean in on God to fill our insecurities. No number of likes, no number of friends, no boyfriend, and no job—nothing—will fill you up like Jesus will. Jesus wants you to be needy; he wants you to be obsessed with him and in love with him. He loves how needy you are. He created every part of you—even the parts you have yet to discover or develop—and he wants your attention.

Jesus is aware of all the things people don't like about you or pick at you about. While we sometimes have parts of ourselves to refine and improve, for the most part, we are perfect just the way God made us!

> "No weapon forged against you will prevail, and you will refute every tongue that accuses you. This is the heritage of the servants of the Lord, and this is their vindication from me," declares the Lord. (Isaiah 54:17)

At the end of the day, who are you trying to impress? Satan is prowling like a lion. Social media is his new playground.

We just spent this time talking about the things within ourselves that we know and pray God reveals for us to improve (Psalm 26:2). In week 7, we asked if you were the type of woman who would attract the man with all the characteristics and attributes you crave in a husband? If that man viewed your social media account, what would he think? Would he block you? Would God block you?

You are a true prophetess. You are called by God to do great things in this world. You are a leader, an encourager, and a lover of good. As you continue to walk in this world as a follower of Jesus, his disciple, let's review what Paul shared a true church leader entails:

> Since an overseer manages God's household, he must be blameless—not overbearing, not quick-tempered, not given to drunkenness, not violent, not pursuing dishonest gain. Rather, he must be hospitable, one who loves what is good, who is self-controlled, upright, holy, and disciplined. He must hold firmly to the trustworthy message as it has been taught, so that he can encourage others by sound doctrine and refute those who oppose it. (Titus 1:7–9)

Hold tight to this verse as you go off into the world, continue to dig into Jesus, and pray and learn the truth of our Savior. If you want respect in this world, if you want to be held to a high standard, then make sure you are honoring every part of your being.

There is evil in this world; be watchful of it and keep your guard up.

In Titus 1:10–16, Paul discusses people who are deceivers, liars, evil, and lazy gluttons.

> Watch and pray so that you will not fall into temptation. The spirit is willing, but the flesh is weak. (Mark 14:38)

Let's pray through these words together:

> Lord, I love the house where you live, the place where your glory dwells. Do not take away my soul along with sinners, my life with those who are bloodthirsty, in whose hands are wicked schemes, whose right hands are full of bribes. I lead a blameless life; deliver me and be merciful to me. My feet stand on level ground; in the great congregation I will praise the Lord. (Psalm 26:12)

Sweet sister, you walk with a God who loves you very much. Hold tight to his commands and use them as a mirror for your life. Hold tight to God's Word and his light. The Holy Spirit resides in your heart. Grasp God's agape love for you with a firm grip.

We are praying for you as you begin your journey of making your faith your own, personalizing this beautiful Bible to your life, unpacking the layers of scripture, and lighting up this world with the love of Jesus Christ!

As we close, let's personalize this verse from Psalm 139:13–16 by inserting your name in the blank; try to commit this verse to memory.

> For you created _____, my inmost being; you knit me, _____, together in my mother's womb. I praise you because I, _____. Am fearfully and wonderfully made; your works are wonderful, I know that full well.

My frame was not hidden from you when I, _____, was made in the secret place, when I was woven together in the depths of the earth. Your eyes saw my uniformed body; all the days ordained for me were written in your book before one of them came to be. (Psalm 139:13–16)

Conclusion

As we close our study this week, we put an end to this ten-session journey we've been on together. Let's reflect on how the Ten Commandments tie perfectly into our lives.

Jesus replied: "'Love the Lord your God with all your heart and with all your soul and with all your mind.' This is the first and greatest commandment. And the second is like it: 'Love your neighbor as yourself.'" (Matthew 22:37–39)

As we just learned, Commandment 10 states, one shall not covet your neighbor's family members, items, and things. Therefore, if we are not loving our one true God and loving our neighbor, we will begin coveting their lives. If we do not believe and trust in the greatest commandments of love, then we leave an opening for all the other nine commandments to fall apart.

In order to stay strong in your walk and portray an image of Christ, you have to be in God's Word. We always have the ability to be grateful, respectful, giving, and nice—even Satan can be nice. Anyone can be nice, but to truly walk with an unending love for God, to look at struggles and praises from a heavenly standpoint, and not earthly, we need to stand firm in our truths and keep filling our minds with God's truth every day.

We are given the Fruits of the Holy Spirit as a guide on how our walk should look; love, joy, peace, patience, kindness, goodness, faithfulness, gentleness, and self-control. (Galatians 5:22)

We challenge you to look into God's mirror daily, lift him up, and ask him to portray anything in your life that needs some fixing. These commandments will help you see and will help you keep your mind clear when culture is filling it with chaos. It's so important to read the Bible for ourselves and then seek Bible teachers when we have questions. All humans fall short of the glory of God—even Bible teachers—so we must dig into the Bible on our own.

We began our study with Psalm 127 and now, as we close, let's remember this beautiful psalm. If we don't cover our lives, our homes, our cars, and our rooms with God, then it is useless.

We have truly enjoyed going through this journey with you, whether we are with you physically or not. We will be personally praying for you; you are loved! We pray you hold tight to your Bible for your truth and refer back to your Blueprint continually. Children are God's best gift—how blessed is God with his quivers full of you, children of God!

> Unless the Lord builds the house, the builders labor in vain.
> Unless the Lord watches over the city, the guards stand watch in vain. In vain you rise early and stay up late,
> toiling for food to eat—for he grants sleep to those he loves.
> Children are a heritage from the Lord, offspring a reward from him.
> Like arrows in the hands of a warrior are children born in one's youth.
> Blessed is the man whose quiver is full of them.
> They will not be put to shame when they contend with their opponents in court. (Psalm 127)

Ladies, sweet children of God, you are the precious daughters and beautiful princesses of the Almighty God! You are royalty!

Prayer

> God, please! Jesus, we lift up all of these beautiful, amazing ladies to you. We ask that you put it deep, deep in their hearts to invite you to guide them through each and every day of their lives. Put a desire in their hearts to build a house with you as their foundation.
> Jesus, please let them feel your security, joy, peace, and love. Let them be forever changed. Let them feel your holy presence upon them and long for it to never leave.
> Please give them a craving to know you so intimately that they become almost obsessed.
> Please bless them with a forever-Christian sister they can confide in, pray with, and cry and laugh with. Let them hold and be held accountable to what they know in their hearts are your desires and plans for them. Thank you, Jesus, for sisterhood.
> Jesus, let them be brave, strong, and determined to take to heart what they have learned and put it all into practice. Protect them from ridicule

and rejection. And if it is indeed your will, Jesus, for them to experience that, let your love numb the sting.

Thank you, Jesus, for your commands and all the lessons you have taught us.

Please let me use it as a tool to keep you the number one focus in my life forever.

In your heavenly name,

Amen

Palm Tree Branches

Scripture Personalized Notecards

Cut out, personalize, add color, add designs, place all around your life, or glue a scripture to one of your journal pages!

Session 1	Session 2
Jesus says, I am the good shepherd; I know _____, and _____ knows me—just as the Father knows me and I know the Father—and I lay down my life for _____. (John 10:14)	Unless the Lord builds _____ house, the builders labor in vain. Unless the Lord watches ove r _____ city, the guards stand watch in vain. In vain you rise early and stay up late, toiling for food to eat— for he grants sleep to _____ whom he loves. (Psalm 127:1–2)
Session 3	Session 4
Do not let any unwholesome talk come out of _____'s mouth, but only what is helpful for building others up according to their needs, that it may benefit those who listen. (Ephesians 4:29)	Yes, _____ soul, finds rest in God; _____ hope comes from him. Truly he is _____ rock and _____ salvation; he is _____ fortress, I will not be shaken. _____ Salvation and _____ honor depend on God; he is my might rock, my refuge. Trust in him at all times, _____; pour out your heart to him, for God is our refuge. (Psalm 62:5–8)

Session 5	Session 6
Let _____ give thanks to the Lord for his unfailing love and his wonderful deeds for humankind. Let _____ sacrifice thank offerings and tell of his works with songs of joy." (Psalm 107:21–22 NIV) Do not let any unwholesome talk come out of _____'s mouth, but only what is helpful for building others up according to their needs, that it may benefit those who listen. (Ephesians 4:29)	_____, put on the full armor of God, so that you can take your stand against the devil's schemes. For _____'s struggle is not against flesh and blood, but against the rulers, against the authorities, against the powers of this dark world, and against the spiritual forces of evil in the heavenly realms. Therefore, _____, put on the full armor of God, so that when the day of evil comes, you may be able to stand your ground, and after you have done everything, to stand. _____, stand firm then with the belt of truth buckled around your waist, with the breastplate of righteousness in place, and with your feet fitted with the readiness that comes from the Gospel of peace. In addition to all this, _____, take up the shield of faith, with which you can extinguish all the flaming arrows of the evil one. (Ephesians 6:11–16)

Session 7	Session 8
Do you not know, _____, that your body is a temple of the Holy Spirit, who is in you, whom you have received from God? You are not your own _____; you were bought at a price. Therefore _____, honor God with your body. (1 Corinthians 6:19–20)	For God so loved _____ that he gave his one and only Son, that whoever believes in him shall not perish but have eternal life. For God did not send his Son into the world to condemn _____, but to save _____ through him. (John 3:16–17)

Session 9	Session 10
_____ brings good things out of the good stored up in her heart, and an evil woman brings evil things out of the evil stored up in her heart. For the mouth speaks what the heart is full of. (Luke 6:45)	For you created _____, my inmost being; you knit me, _____, together in my mother's womb. I praise you because I, _____, am fearfully and wonderfully made; your works are wonderful, I know that full well. My frame was not hidden from you when I, _____, was made in the secret place, when I was woven together in the depths of the earth. Your eyes saw my uniformed body; all the days ordained for me were written in your book before one of them came to be. (Psalm 139:13–16)

APPENDIX 1

Self-Esteem Quiz

Read the questions below, make a check next to each question that applies to you, tear out of your BP, and hand to your coach. (Do not add your name.)

Facilitators: Once you have collected the finished quizzes, mix them up, hand them back out to the students, and read off each question. If the students have a check next to that question, have them raise their hand.

This thought crosses your mind from time to time: "My friends are prettier than I am."

I feel like people get sick of listening to me.

Sometimes I feel like I talk too much.

I sometimes wish my body looked different (skinnier, more muscle, or a flatter stomach).

I wish I had better hair.

I feel like my peers are more talented than I am.

I feel like my friends have better style than me (clothing, shoes, earrings, makeup etc.).

Sometimes, I can't stand myself.

I often compromise my integrity to fit it.

I frequently compare myself to others.

I judge my worth by the people I hang out with.

I tend to think more negatively about myself than positively.

I spend too much time worrying about how I look.

I feel angry about myself if I make a mistake—even if it is an honest mistake.

It bothers me considerably when others disapprove of me.

I usually go along with the group—even if I don't really agree.

Printed in the United States
By Bookmasters